Curt Simmons

JESUS
The Man
The Majesty
The Model

ILLUMINATION PUBLISHERS

About the author: Curt Simmons is a native of the state of Washington and received his degree in Journalism from Western Washington University. He has served in the full-time ministry since 1982, working in nine different states and two countries. Curt has been married to his wife, Patty, for 40 years, and they have two children and five grandchildren. They live in Chicago where they work with the Chicago Church of Christ. Curt is the author of four other books, *The Unveiling, Small-Town Heroes, The Brotherhood of Believers* and *Unsung Heroes: The Mack Strong Story.*

ILLUMINATION PUBLISHERS   www.ipibooks.com

Contents

The Man, the Majesty, the Model

I suppose, in some way, a revised version of this book I wrote seventeen years ago was inevitable. Perhaps that's mostly because it's a book about Jesus. In the forty years I've been making it my goal to learn as much about Jesus as possible and imitate him as much as possible, I've discovered that I'm constantly revising my own life to keep it more in step with his. And I've also come to discover that Jesus is way more awesome than what I thought he was back then. Now that's not because Jesus has somehow improved during that span of time. You can't improve upon perfection. Rather it has been my spiritual awareness that has grown, and that awareness has translated into greater insight regarding this one remarkable individual.

So it makes sense to me that I would also look back at my writing about Jesus from 2005 and find some ways that it, too, could and should be modified and improved upon. And that's exactly what I've done. Though much of the book is quite similar to the first edition, I've done a few things to set it apart from its initial publication.

First, it's considerably shorter, about sixty pages or so. Not that I think the content in those pages was stocked with inaccurate or insufficient information on Jesus, but more because of the times we live in—where less seems to be of greater appeal than more. Most people these days are looking for the fastest way to gain the most amount of information, so hopefully this edition will provide that opportunity in a better way than the first.

I've also changed this, the introduction, to bring readers up to speed on a few things that have happened in my life since 2005 and how knowing the real Jesus helped me navigate those uncharted waters.

Now if you've already read the first version of this book, I think a refresher course on Jesus is always a healthy choice to make on one's spiritual journey. Personally, I can never get enough of Jesus. I just finished reading a book about Jesus that's definitely one of my favorites, entitled *The Jesus I Never Knew* by Philip Yancey. I think that was my third or fourth time reading it, but it seemed very new and fresh to me, and I came away from reading it with an even greater appreciation and admiration of Jesus. I hope the same will happen for you if this is a repeat endeavor. But if this is your first time, I'm glad you've decided to take a look at Jesus from my perspective. I think what you'll discover will be well worth the investment of your time.

Lastly, I've decided to change the main title of the book while keeping the subtitle. While *The Revealer* (the old title) does indicate what I believe Jesus came to do—reveal God in human form—this time I wanted the name Jesus to be front and center on the cover. The subtitle of "the man, the majesty and the model" I'm sticking with because I believe those three "titles" are essential to understanding Jesus in a complete way. He was fully human (*the man*). He was fully divine, fully God (*the majesty*). And without a doubt, he has fully earned the right to be followed (*the model*)—to be the absolute, one and only, perfect example for our individual lives. Any teaching that doesn't bestow on Jesus the right to these three claims is false and heretical in every possible way.

Being fully human (*the man*), I take great comfort in knowing that Jesus is well aware of the challenges I face in my day-to-day existence. And when I find myself thinking God is clueless about how difficult life on this planet can be at times, I'm reminded of this wonderful truth— *In the beginning was the Word; and the Word was with God and the Word was God…And the Word became flesh and dwelt among us* (**John 1:1-2, 14**). And as the Hebrew writer declares: *For this reason, he had to be made like them, fully human in every way, in order that he might become a merciful and faithful high priest in service to God, and that he might make atonement for the sins of the people. Because he himself suffered when he was tempted, he is able to help those who are being tempted* (**Hebrews 2:17-18**).

Being fully divine (*the majesty*), I take great comfort in knowing I have a perfectly powerful and capable king who can lead me to victory after victory over the invisible forces of evil. Jesus is Lord of lords and King of kings, and therefore I have absolutely nothing to fear or worry about in my walk through life. Jesus has me in his sights at all times. He has a perfect plan mapped out for me to arrive safely to his eternal kingdom in heaven. And most importantly, he is the one (and the only one) who has the ability to offer me and provide for me what I need the most in order to get there—much grace and mercy.!

How Jesus was fully human and fully divine remains a mystery to me and many others. But God has always been known to go "off the grid" and do things that leave us breathless and tongue-tied. In my flesh, I can't fully comprehend this great mystery, but that doesn't make it any less true. What I see and hear in Jesus as revealed in the Scriptures can only be summed up in one way—God was definitely here on planet Earth for a brief visit and left his indelible mark on history.

Jesus being (*the model*) makes total sense once you come to believe those first two truths. If Jesus is fully man and fully God, why wouldn't we watch him closely and do our best to imitate him? Why wouldn't we want to model our lives after the one who never sinned? Why wouldn't we keep striving to be better disciples in the hope we can inch closer and closer to the perfect pattern Jesus left for each of us.

As you're reading, I want to encourage you to notice these three emphases and how they come alive in Jesus. Take note of **the man, the majesty and the model** as much as possible. Stand in awe of what you see, then commit (or recommit) to doing everything in your power to walk as he walked (**1 John 2:5-6**) and worship him as he so richly deserves (**John 20:15-16**).

Two events in my life the previous seventeen years have reminded me of the great importance of relying on these truths about Jesus.

The first of those happened over a period of about five years from 2004-2009 when I suffered from an undiagnosed illness that greatly minimized my energy levels and caused significant imbalance issues. From a misdiagnosis of cancer in the early stages of my illness, to a wrong diagnosis (from a doctor at a well-respected hospital) claiming that it was all in my head and that I was faking my symptoms, I needed Jesus desperately. I needed to know he could understand the myriad of feelings and emotions I encountered during that time—anger, desperation, loneliness, worry, frustration, resignation and self-pity, just to name a few—and that he was powerful enough and could distribute some of that power to me so I could endure it all.

I also needed to be reminded that Jesus was still my model for how to behave in the middle of all those feelings and emotions, and that I couldn't lower the bar on righteous behavior during that scary, long-lasting storm. Jesus provided for me a clear picture of staying strong and steadfast in the midst of chaos and crises, and those examples were a great inspiration (and correction) for me on a regular basis. Thankfully, my illness was properly diagnosed in the latter part of 2008. Turns out it had to do with a birth defect (*pectus excavatum*), one that I was obviously well aware that I had. But I wasn't aware of the worsening effects that aging brought with it, and I had no idea that my defect was one of the worst cases the experts in that condition had ever seen. But after two successful reconstruction surgeries and about a year of recovery, I was back to normal.

The second way I found this threefold description of Jesus to be quite helpful was from 2015-2018 when my wife and I served as missionaries in Eastern Europe. We spent much of that time working with a church in Warsaw, Poland, and other shorter stays in places like Istanbul, Turkey; Bucharest, Romania; Tirana, Albania; and Zagreb, Croatia. While it was such a great experience, those four years were difficult on many fronts—numerous visa issues that didn't allow us to stay in one place longer than three months; the daunting challenge of trying (emphasis on trying) to learn another language, Polish in this case, one of the most difficult languages for English speakers to learn; dealing with little or no numerical growth in the churches we were overseeing; being separated from family and having our first two grandchildren born while we were away; and just simply missing the comforts of home in the good ole' USA. But these three truths about Jesus provided us the comfort and direction we desperately needed.

Jesus could relate on so many levels. He, too, was away from the comforts of his home—heaven. He too, was always on the go in his ministry, and he didn't seem to be too concerned about it. Three months in one place for Jesus would have been a luxury! He, too, was speaking a new language instead of the heavenly one he spoke fluently. He, too, dealt at times with poor results in convincing people to follow him. All of that and more made it quite easy to connect with Jesus on our missionary journeys. But knowing that Jesus was not just a man but majesty as well gave me the confidence to know that all would be okay, and that I should just focus on continuing to do what was right to the best of my ability. And the model Jesus displayed for having the proper attitude while in a foreign place and away from the comforts of home, as well as righteously dealing with the disappointment and discouragement that can come from a lack of ministry success—all of that and more helped to keep me on the right track consistently.

Other challenging times (and good times) that have occurred over the past seventeen years of my life have also steered me to this three-fold description of Jesus. And no doubt there will be many more life situations that will bring me back to these truths about Jesus during my remaining years.

My prayer is that these three wonderful truths about Jesus will give you everything you need during your times of trial or triumph. Certainly you will have both throughout your life. And Jesus will be there to guide you safely through them all. With that in mind, keep reading and watch Jesus in action. I think you will like what you see!

In the past, God spoke to our ancestors through the prophets at many times and in various ways, but in these last days he has spoken to us by his Son, whom he appointed heir of all things, and through whom also he made the universe.

–Hebrews 1:1-2

CHAPTER ONE

May I Have Your Attention, Please?

Good luck trying to get anybody's undivided attention these days. Most of the people we try to turn in our direction aren't that interested in our interruptions, even if it's only for a brief time or for a noble purpose. If we dare try, we should be prepared to get laughed at, left alone or both. But before we start pointing too many fingers, this is likely how most of us would react if people tried barging into our busy lives!

Nobody has dealt with this dilemma more often than God. From the beginning, God has dangled eye-popping masterpieces in people's plain sight, hoping they will stop, marvel and make it their mission to get to know the artist. Granted, a small percentage of folks do actually slow down for a moment in their fast-paced lives and thank God for his magnificent artwork. A few even get acquainted with the artist, learning from him and looking for opportunities to introduce him to others. Unfortunately, the vast majority of men and women don't do either. They're just really busy.

God's attention-getters started with his mind-blowing, awe-inspiring, "wow"-inducing, six-day spectacular called creation—all of it designed to make it unbelievably easy to believe in a creator and worship him accordingly (**Romans 1:18-25**).

A never-ending sky that beautifully canopies the Earth by day and marvelously shrinks it by night reveals God's never-ending nature.

Ocean waves that rarely overflow their boundaries speak of a God who regularly and willingly restrains himself with invisible shorelines called grace and mercy to keep humans from drowning in their sin.

Majestic mountains rising miles above the Earth are reminders of God's powerful and immoveable nature, calling out for all who view them or climb them to stand in awe and stand at attention.

The towering trees that fill the forests and spread their branches to provide shade for mankind tell of a God who reaches out to his creation and who can keep them from collapsing in the sweltering heat called daily living.

The bright, blazing sun is a constant reminder that light is available from above, that something so far away and so unreachable can still make its way to the Earth and shine on every inch of its surface. A power that, though it can't always be seen, can always be felt.

The moon and countless stars placed in the expanse above are reminders that, even in the midst of humanity's darkness, light is available from the heavens.

The changing of the Earth's guard every twenty-four hours proclaims God's trustworthy nature and provides a continual opportunity for everybody to realize he loves the idea of a fresh start.

The clouds delivering rain to water the Earth and irrigate the planted fields speak of God's desire to bring food to people's tables and freshness for their wilting lives.

Lightning makes individuals run for cover in fear, yet in the same moment helps them realize that power is available in an instant and transferrable from heaven to Earth.

The rainbow affords everyone the opportunity to marvel at the beauty of God, stand in awe of the colors of creation and better comprehend the creativity and diversity of their Maker.

And this is just a small sampling of the many messages God has left in his creation of the universe to *send out his voice to the ends of the world* (**Psalm 19:1-6**). From the beginning, however, most humans haven't been very good listeners. But God continued to speak, at times raising his powerful voice to give men and women more chances to get things right. Sometimes it was a "watch out below" warning. At other times, it was a "way to go" word of encouragement.

For example, in the days of Noah, God spoke of rainy days to come, then brought a worldwide flood of cataclysmic proportions to warn all human beings that continual evil without a corresponding choice to repent would ultimately bring horrific consequences (**Genesis 6:5-13**).

He confused the one universal language during the Tower of Babel fiasco to teach mankind that prideful thoughts, pointless pursuits and putting off his original plan to populate the entire Earth would not be tolerated (**Genesis 11:1-9**).

He dropped ten devastating plagues upon a top world power to illustrate the absurdity of arrogance and idolatry (**Exodus 7-12**).

God raised up Israel, a tiny and inexperienced gathering of sinful people to display to the rest of the world that enormous benefits come from worshiping and listening to him (**Deuteronomy 9:1-6**).

He stopped the regular rotation of the Earth and made the sun stand still for an entire day to show he had absolute control over the every-day affairs of mankind and would go to great lengths to bless his people (**Joshua 10:1-14**).

He sent prophet after prophet, again and again, to tell his chosen people and those on the outside that, though his love was constant and his patience extreme, his expectations were still to be honored (**Jeremiah 25:1-7**).

He later disciplined Israel and banished them to exile, reminding them and the rest of the world that his covenant benefits ended when commitment to him ended (**2 Chronicles 36:15-19**).

These are just a few illustrations of what God did to encourage men and women of old to seek him, find him and stay with him as we watch the drama played out in the biblical record following the six-day creation spectacular. Who knows how many other messages God sent to Earth throughout the early centuries to lift eyes and hearts heavenward. God was constantly revealing truths about himself and his expectations. But because people were really busy, and because their desires were centered elsewhere, most didn't fully comprehend him or care much for submitting to him.

Then God spoke his loudest and clearest. For thirty-three years, he lived in a small area in what we know today as the Middle East and spent most of his time with a dozen ordinary and unschooled men who were willing to listen to him—proving his deity with compelling messages, breathtaking miracles and remarkable acts of kindness. He called himself Jesus. In Jesus, God personally introduced himself to mankind. He revealed his love, his power, his goodness, his patience, his expectations, his judgments and, most importantly, his directions for obtaining a personal relationship with him and a permanent home with him.

Though he had every right to do it, God didn't give up on people. And he didn't wait for the "really busy" folks to free up their schedules and start seeking him. Instead, he humbly stepped down from his heavenly throne, started off in a womb like the rest of us and began his life as Jesus—God in a human body.

No, you and I weren't there to see him face to face or hear him speak. But the written revelation of Jesus' activity on Earth is just as good. As a matter of fact, it's probably even better! Now we get to see and hear so much more of Jesus than those in the first century, other than the twelve apostles and a few other fortunate individuals who were granted additional time with him.

As I see it, those of us living today have an added bonus and are blessed with what I call the "trio of testimony" when it comes to God's revealing nature. First, we still have daily viewings of *the creation*. And we have so many more opportunities to marvel at it than those who lived even a few decades ago, thanks to travel options and technology. Second, we still have access to *the collection of Scriptures* and all the events God chose to have recorded in the Old Testament. And finally, we get to see Jesus, *the Christ*, up close and personal in the pages of the New Testament. Of all people throughout history, we have the best shot at gaining a full understanding and appreciation of God.

So let me encourage you to push "Pause" on your really busy life and spend some time taking a trip back in time to hear what God had to say—through Jesus this time. As you do, you'll push "Play" and discover (or rediscover) the one person God was preparing his creation to meet, even before creation and the time of Adam and Eve, and the one he's been proudly pointing people to the past two-thousand years. It is to this one man whom we all must give our utmost attention.

*No one has ever seen God, but the one
and only Son, who is himself God and is in
closest relationship with the Father,
has made him known.*

–John 1:18

CHAPTER TWO

Final Statement

In addition to the creation signs and the many warnings and encouragements God provided in the centuries to follow, he also left a number of convincing clues as to his identity and his feelings for mankind in the hundreds of pages we have come to know as the Old Testament. During this time, he used prophets to relay specific messages about who he was and what he expected. He enabled many of those individuals to perform miraculous signs to confirm that the words they were speaking were not of human origin but had been sent from another realm.

God tried on numerous occasions to let his chosen people know he was immediately available for them and wanted what was best for their lives, looking for them to then relay those same glorious truths to the general population. He revealed his Ten Commandments on Mount Sinai to Moses. He unveiled his failsafe wisdom on a number of key life topics through King Solomon in the books of Proverbs and Ecclesiastes. And he encouraged Daniel and the exiled nation of Israel by showing them magnificent scenes of the future. God was constantly speaking and making sure his truths would be recorded and preserved for generations to come. Unfortunately, many of those who gained access to his written word chose not to read it at all, or they read it with an arrogant mindset as though it were optional to believe or practice. So God did what had been a part of his true character for all eternity and what had been a part of his plan for all eternity—he went the second mile and came to deliver the word in person. Truly, the Word became flesh.

God himself entered a womb and entered time, all the while still upholding the universe. He did so in the person of Jesus Christ—*the radiance of God's glory and the exact representation of his being* (**Hebrews 1:3**). Jesus did things and said things during one short time-span of history to get man's absolute attention. God was shouting long and loud through Jesus because he knew he wasn't going to say it again. So what we have in Jesus is God's final statement. Everything written up to that point was pointing to him. Everything written after Jesus' arrival looked back to his activity on Earth. You might say Jesus stopped the heavenly printing presses. Perfection had arrived in the flesh, and he was the final headline, story, advertisement and editorial in God's final edition.

The information presented about Jesus in the Scriptures is therefore essential for everyone to know and believe. God will not say anything else about the subject that he hasn't already revealed. He won't send you a personal message on Facebook or Twitter, or write additional insights in the formation of the clouds or in the cream of your morning coffee. Jesus has spoken, and now it's your job and mine to just listen.

What exactly did Jesus say and do that is all-sufficient for all mankind? What important life lessons might someone discover by discovering him? Why is there no pressing need for God to send another messenger? What do we see in Jesus that should remind us to no longer look for additional information from heaven? And is Jesus really the all-time, undisputed champion of spiritual truth as he claimed to be?

Some of my fondest memories growing up are centered around the times my father and I would sit in our living room watching professional wrestling on Saturday nights, as well as the few times we watched it live in our ringside seats, cheering and jeering as the acrobatic behemoths pounded on each other. But it wasn't until I was about fourteen that I realized it was much more show than real competition.

Everything I was seeing looked so incredibly real. My unsuspicious eyes and overly-trusting heart saw it that way. Many people were trying to convince me otherwise, but surely they were just misinformed or hadn't been watching the action as closely as me. Even in person it looked to be authentic. Once while sitting at ringside, one of the wrestlers grabbed a chair in our row and began walloping his opponent repeatedly on the top of his head. Blood was gushing everywhere. And oh, you better believe it—that was real blood. I could tell with my own two eyes that those blows were definitely landing and no doubt causing a great deal of bodily damage. That 350-pound champion descending spread-eagle in mid air from atop the turnbuckle most definitely land-ed with full force on the mid-section of his dazed enemy lying helpless on the mat. Oh yes, my friend, it was one-hundred percent legit—without a doubt. Those were top-notch athletes and fierce competitors in the truest sense. My eyes saw it. My heart felt it. And even if nobody else was smart enough to see it that way, I was always going to believe it and stick up for my heroes who were claiming nothing was staged and that the outcome of each match was left up to the man with the brawn and the best moves.

It wasn't too long after my fourteenth birthday that I turned on the television one Saturday night and noticed that a punch to the head of an opposing wrestler, sending him flailing to the mat, never actually touched him. My wrestling world was rocked, and I realized that what I had been defending the past few years was simply a product of my youthful and misguided zeal. So with great hesitation and much trembling of heart, I swallowed massive doses of humble pie and finally admitted what family and friends had been telling me for years.

It's now almost fifty years later, and professional wrestling hasn't changed a bit. Only the names are new—those Goliaths in tights exciting their diehard fans and entertaining millions around the world. I'll occasionally catch a few moments while channel-surfing, and it's quite easy to see through the deception of those finely-tuned athletes and entertainers. How come it wasn't so easy to spot it back when I could have used the information to avoid high levels of ridicule from fellow eighth-graders?

It's my firm conviction that professional wrestlers and Jesus Christ have very little in common when it comes to their time on stage. Jesus was the real deal. Unfortunately, many today don't see it that way and look at Jesus as just another entertainer for those who are into the religious thing.

But where do you stand with Jesus at this point in your life? Is he the real deal, and are all those glorious accolades we hear attributed to him truly deserved? Or is he simply a figment of our religious imagination, cleverly contrived over the centuries so Christians can shout, "My God's better than your God!"? Or are you willing to admit Jesus actually lived, but then conclude nobody could be that awesome? Surely some of his followers got caught up in the moment and then got carried away writing his biography. What do you think?

Regardless of your current beliefs concerning Jesus, I hope this book serves as a private viewing of some of the toughest matches he entered. When the film starts rolling, you'll notice that every blow Jesus aimed at the enemy actually landed square, and the blood seen running down the entire body of the champion is very real indeed. It will become obvious that every opponent Jesus faced wasn't faking anything or surrendering to him without a fight to the finish. You'll discover that the undefeated and untied record throughout his entire career was definitely earned. You'll be especially impressed after reviewing his final match on Earth as Jesus looked certain to surrender his championship belt after being knocked out cold and thrown onto the stadium floor—only to be revived just short of being pinned by the count of three and coming out of nowhere to score his greatest victory.

My prayer is that this look at Jesus in the ring called planet Earth, and seeing how he fought and gained a convincing victory against the powerful forces of evil, will help to open your eyes and your heart to the truth that has always been truth—Jesus is God's eternal champion and the messenger he sent to deliver his final statement.

Jesus did many other things as well. If every one of them were written down, I suppose that even the whole world would not have room for the books that would be written.

—John 21:25

CHAPTER THREE

Other Things

The final statement God made in written form concerning Jesus is actually fairly brief. Quite fitting, you might say, for the really busy people we are and have been ever since he came! God could have left us with hundreds of memoirs recording the life of Jesus. But he gave us only four—Matthew, Mark, Luke and John—chosen instruments of God used to capture enough moments in the life of Jesus to impress us, instruct us and inspire us. These men have told us the story of the Son of God. Jesus did many other things while he was here, yet only these were recorded and preserved in the Scriptures. What else might we have come to know about Jesus if everything concerning this remarkable man had been revealed?

No doubt there were many other paralyzed and demon-possessed people who crossed his path and were miraculously healed.

Surely more attention-grabbing parables were presented and eye-opening sermons were delivered.

How many others went from overwhelming sadness to ongoing smiles when Jesus brought back breath to a deceased loved one?

How many hundreds of ten-minute, life-changing conversations did Jesus have with the previously misguided that are missing from the written word?

How many thousands of ten-second, "You're important to me" moments do you suppose Jesus handed out during his time on Earth?

How many lives were changed by his "I'm happy to see you" smile or his "I know exactly what you're thinking" stare?

How much more amazed would we be if every one of Jesus' early-morning prayer times or late-night rendezvous with God had been recorded?

What other reading material could we have enjoyed that detailed his follow-up visits with all the deaf and blind individuals he healed?

What about a book for each of Jesus' one-on-one evangelistic endeavors and his reaction to their reaction?

What were Jesus' innermost thoughts during his nights of sleeping outdoors as he stared at the stars he had made?

How about some recorded insight on how Jesus dealt with each of the temptations he faced during his teenage years?

What were his private conversations with Judas all about?

How many deathbed discussions did Jesus have with people he knew were on the verge of ending up in hell? What did Jesus say to them? Did any of them respond and repent? Were there any forerunners to the thief on the cross and his remarkable change of heart (**Luke 23:32-43**)?

How about some additional information concerning all the undocumented discipleship groups with his apostles? How many other times did Jesus gather the group of twelve to dam their flood of selfishness (**Matthew 20:20-28**)?

When did Jesus cry when nobody was watching, and what was it that moved him to tears?

What made Jesus laugh? What were his most humorous moments?

What did Jesus do in his spare time? What were his hobbies?

Did he ever have a follow-up talk with the rich, young ruler to give him one more chance to accept his offer (**Matthew 19:16-26**)?

What did Jesus think and feel as he washed the dirt from the feet of Judas (**John 13:1-17**)? What did he feel right after that same man's infamous kiss of betrayal (**Matthew 26:47-50**)?

These questions and others you might be asking are all very interesting. We can venture a guess at all of them, but nobody knows the absolute answer to any of them. In his divine wisdom, God chose not to reveal them. Sure, the "other things" are fun to imagine, discuss or even debate, and we'll spend a little time in the book doing just that, especially in Chapters 14 and 15. But none of these "other things" are essential to know. The revealed things are!

Thank God he has chosen to leave us plenty of relevant information about Jesus in these four accounts. And if we commit to discovering his heart, his actions and his expectations, and if we make it our number one ambition to imitate him in every way, it will keep us occupied and on target for the rest of our lives.

*Dear friends, do not believe every spirit,
but test the spirits to see whether they are
from God, because many false prophets
have gone out into the world.*

−1 John 4:1

CHAPTER FOUR

To Tell the Truth

Will the real Jesus Christ please stand up?

The show was *To Tell the Truth,* and four all-star panelists were given one simple task—find the fakes! Two of the three contestants they questioned were liars. Only one actually was who they said they were and actually did what they said they did.

The phonies were fully primed. They knew a lot about the truth-teller and, without conscience, looked forward to their job of deception. Show regulars Bill Cullen and Kitty Carlisle joined two other panelists on a six-minute exploration for truth, each being allowed 90 seconds to engage in some serious probing of the contestants. Could they catch a pretender off-guard? Was a stuttered answer a dead giveaway? Was a pause or hesitation a sign of panic from the fake or a decoy from the truth-teller? Did one-word answers stem from a lack of deeper knowledge, or were they purposely succinct to throw off the questioner?

When the interrogations were complete, the ballots were cast. Who did Kitty select? Did Bill go with his gut or just guess? Every night, host Garry Moore would pose the same question to the trios: "Will the real *John Brown* please stand up?" Down to the very end, the three suspects left the panel and millions of truth-seekers glued to their television sets wondering. Often, the impersonators would rise from their seats as if to answer the all-important question, only to sit down again while the man with the proper identification rose and acknowledged his honesty.

Those were always an exciting thirty minutes for my family. Each night I battled with fellow *To Tell the Truth* loyalists in the room and had a good time guessing. Like the panelists, I won some, lost some. And now, nearly fifty years later, I've been watching the latest version of this classic game show that has made a comeback of sorts. And though the general format is somewhat different now from what it was way back then, the premise is much the same. And so are my personal results. I win some, lose some.

Now you're the panelist and it's time to decide. Who is Jesus Christ? What was he like? What did he believe? What did he teach? Do you really know him, or are you just guessing? Would you be shocked to see the real Jesus rising from his throne? Would you have selected him?

What would the actual Jesus say about the present condition of the world? More importantly, what would he say about the present condition of your life?

What would he teach about possessions, sacrifice, the stock market and other money matters?

How would he deal with an unexpected traffic delay or the slow-moving vehicle in the fast lane?

How would Jesus react to a flirtatious woman given the opportunity for a one-on-one, nobody's watching interaction with her?

Would he be ticked with taxes, and how would he fill out his IRS forms?

What would Jesus do in a crisis and how would he get out of a jam?

Would he ever bypass a beggar? What kind of conversation would he strike up with that individual?

How often would Jesus pray, read the Scriptures and attend religious gatherings?

What would he do with constant interruptions?

How would he handle humans who were blame-shifting and bellyaching?

Who would his heroes be today? For what and for whom would he reserve his greatest applause?

What would he hate? How would he communicate that hatred?

How would he feel about social and racial injustice? How would he choose to express those feelings?

How would he deal with poor customer service? How would he respond when the service was stellar?

What type of information would Jesus post on social media?

What would his stance be on living together before marriage, a lousy marriage and leaving a marriage?

What would he think about boss-bashing and general disrespect for authority?

How would he respond to mask and vaccine mandates, social distancing guidelines and all the other changes and challenges a worldwide pandemic brings?

What would his platform be in regard to negative political campaigns and the awful way candidates for public office often speak about each other?

What would characterize his discussions concerning the LGBTQ+ community?

What would characterize his discusssions with the LGBTQ+ community?

Where would Jesus land on the issues of abortion, immigration and gun-control?

How would Jesus deal with physical pain, persistent pressure, persecution and praise from others?

What do you think? Do you know the answers to these questions?

The real Jesus Christ is there for all of us to see. Unfortunately, so are the deceivers—Satan's servants looking to tickle your ears, trip you up, take you down, turn your life into unmanageable chaos and tear up your ticket to the heavenly reunion. Thank God you have more than a few minutes to get it right. If you're in your twenties, you've already been given about ten-million of them—precious minutes that could have been spent pointing you to the Son of God. Have you capitalized? Have you taken the time to discover the inside scoop into this man's personal history?

Introducing Jesus Christ—a flesh and blood verification of what God had said to mankind for thousands of years prior to his arrival—I love you completely, I want you to know me intimately and I want you to move in with me permanently. Jesus was the God-Man with the glorious message—"I'll go all out for you and give you all you need to go all out for me."

God desperately wants you to know Jesus Christ. Without knowing Jesus and making a decision to live for him, you'll face some challenging situations in the days ahead that likely won't make much sense to you. When they come, and if you're unable to understand them in their proper context, they will greatly complicate matters in your already complicated life. Or as is the case most of the time, they will steal the joy God has intended for you and the salvation he has marked out for you. Neither is worth forfeiting.

Could some knowledge of Jesus bring you the long-awaited perspective on life that may have escaped you to this point? Could an inside look at how he handled his own pressures and how he dealt with people in your shoes two-thousand years ago convince you that he's still capable of rescuing you from your perils today? Could Jesus be the vehicle you need while traveling in this dark and dangerous world? Is he the Hummer you should purchase before the next crash in your life occurs? Or can you be just as confident and secure riding in a Hyundai or a Honda?

Can a closer look at the life of Jesus help you to determine how to best go about starting a new relationship or restoring a broken one? Can his activity on Earth teach you anything about the activities you'll need to participate in while trying to bring joy and excitement into your life?

God is absolutely thrilled to let you and the whole world know about his Son. He works to give every human being a chance to know of his days on Earth, his deeds for mankind, his death on a cross, his delivery from the threshold of death and his duties ever since that remarkable escape. God delights in Jesus Christ. He longs to show him off. He wants his entire history to be a public spectacle. God isn't embarrassed by a single moment or hiding a single flaw. He is righteously proud of the plan and eager to divulge it.

You and I are simply 21st-century panelists on a spiritual *To Tell the Truth*, looking for the man who boldly claimed to be the Son of God.

Will the real Jesus Christ please stand up?

*Watch out that no one deceives you.
For many will come in my name, claiming,
"I am the Christ," and will deceive many.*

—Matthew 24:4-5

CHAPTER FIVE

The Great Impostor

I met Ferdinand (Fred) Demara in 1968 when I was nine years old. He was a robust man with a Santa Claus smile and always found time to make me feel special. He was a minister for the one and only church in the small, logging town of Toutle, Washington where I lived from the third grade until my high school graduation. Reverend Demara (as most referred to him) was well liked and respected and would show up for most of the significant community events. One of the most important of those appearances for me was at my older brother's funeral in 1969, as he was one of the men who spoke during the memorial. I don't remember any of the content of his message that day, but I do remember feeling like he really cared. And he continued to express his concern for my family's emotional welfare with his many visits to our home following my brother's death.

Demara moved away from Toutle about a year after my brother's passing. And though our family kept in contact with him for a few years after his departure, my recollection of him ended around age twelve. But his life had great impact on more than just one child who had lost his big brother. Much of the positive impact from Demara's life came after a dramatic turnaround of his troubled younger days that ultimately landed him in church work. Demara's hard-to-track trail of deceit became headline news across America beginning in the late 1940s and stretching into the early 1960s, and the story of his life was soon developed into a Hollywood movie with Tony Curtis in the starring role. Fred Demara was better known as "The Great Impostor."

An intense, all-out manhunt led to Demara's arrest and ultimate conviction in 1961, though he spent very little actual time behind bars for his crimes. In his more-than-a-decade reign as America's greatest con-artist, Demara was Dr. Joseph C. Cyr, surgeon lieutenant in the Royal Canadian Navy; Ben Jones, assistant warden of the Huntsville Prison in Texas; Dr. Robert Lincoln French, head of a college psychology department; and Brother M. Jerome, novitiate in a Trappist monastery, just to name a few.

Demara performed admirably at each position, including successful surgeries as a naval doctor, making it even more difficult to detect the hidden truth. He had accumulated very convincing documents for each of the men he impersonated and, through what he called the naivety of man, became perhaps the boldest impostor the world had ever known. In the book, *The Great Impostor: The Amazing Careers of the Most Spectacular Impostor of Modern Times,* Demara shared the secrets of his success in weaving his way into even the most challenging of positions. For example, consider his following thoughts on the basic strategies of being a good doctor:

> "The seriously sick know they're sick, and so do you. Those you send to a hospital. The rest are all going to get better sooner or later, and anything you do for them will seem right. And because they think you're a doctor, they automatically feel better."

Demara's successful reign as The Great Impostor was a clear indication that those in charge of the hiring process weren't looking closely enough into important matters. He lived out his many lies with forged, stolen or non-existent qualifications. Exhaustive background checks with corresponding photographs and eyewitness confirmations of identity were deemed unimportant by those in a position to hire him. The many worlds he ventured into needed immediate help, and Demara was always there to oblige.

The world we live in is the same arena Satan and the spiritual forces of evil have been allowed to temporarily occupy (**Revelation**

12:7-12). It's a world with billions of people crying loud and often for help. Echoes of "Fix me God," "Heal me God" and "Save me God" have Satan and his cleverly disguised demons rushing to the doorsteps of these desperate souls, ready to offer them a delightful array of quick-fix Messiahs. "You're fixed," "You're healed" and "You're saved" are the promises being made to those looking for the simplest and most satisfying salvation scenarios.

But our world also has billions of people who would be very interested in following the real Jesus, only they can't get past those recurring thoughts of "I can't change," "I've never been successful at anything in life" and "I'm not good enough anyway." Satan and his henchmen are quite eager to agree with them. "You're beyond fixing," "You'll never make it anyway" and "You aren't worth saving" are a few of the lies those God-haters love to plant in the hearts and minds of men and women who remain trapped in the basement of their skyscraper called self-esteem.

The biggest problem with both of these presentations is that there's no biblical basis for either. But most of the selfish seekers don't really seem to care about hearing any hard-and-fast evidence or biblical proof on the new position with God they're being promised. Too much information might just take away the warm and fuzzy feelings they need to continue wading through their shallow lives.

"That Jesus sounds so good to me, who would ever turn him down?"

Sadly, those searching for self-worth and a place to belong tend to believe the hellish lies just as quickly after receiving confirmation of their total unworthiness. Then they retreat with their heads hanging low to dark, yet familiar dungeons of "I knew I couldn't cut it" and "Why did I get my hopes up again?"

"That Jesus sounds so intense, who would ever be able to follow him?"

Unfortunately, too many people are either following the wrong Messiah or their interest in following the right one has plummeted to an all-time low.

So let's take some time and see if we can spot some of the defective "Messiah merchandise" on the market. You've probably encountered some of it while watching the "Jesus Goes to Hollywood" blockbusters casting the frail and effeminate man with a British accent in the starring role. Others you may have been introduced to while tuning in to Sunday morning church services from the comfort of your bed. Or maybe you remember meeting the one in Sunday school who spent most of his time smiling for no apparent reason. Or the one talking softly to thousands of people on the mountainside who are supposedly hearing and hanging on his every word. Or perhaps it's the one petting the precious lamb lying on his lap. Or maybe the one you identify with the most is the one wearing the permanent scowl. Or the Jesus who's looking a bit dazed and confused—his head completely in the clouds and acting as though this visit to Earth strategy was a big mistake. Or maybe none of these apply to you, but you've developed your impression of Jesus from secular books, best friends or out-of-context Bible verses.

Whatever the case, here are some frequently spotted impostors of Jesus who've been set free from the gates of hell. In regard to the first seven impostors we'll meet, most of us would find them very attractive. The last five are all unbelievably ugly. All twelve are false.

First, let's look at the product for sale. Then we'll listen to the Satanic sales pitch that follows.

Impostor #1: *The Believe What You Want to Believe About Me Just As Long As You Believe Jesus*

"After all, it wouldn't be like a loving Savior to shove truth down your throat. If you want him to be Lord of *all* your life, he'll oblige. If not, he'll be happy for the few areas you allow him to control. So you think he is *the* Son of God? Great! He would actually settle for something less. Is Confucius your cup of tea? Go ahead and drink, just sip on Jesus every now and then. Is Mohammed more of what you're looking for in a Messiah? Jesus is perfectly fine with that, just as long as he can be found in your top three."

Impostor #2: *The Everyone Is Going to Heaven Anyway Jesus*

"Wasn't the main purpose for Jesus' arrival to get you to heaven and not necessarily to expect you to embrace his morals or choose his better way of living? Sure, you'd probably improve your quality of life eventually if you did things his way. But right now, you look like you need some freedom from religion, and those "deny yourself" statements are probably better off denied. Thank God Jesus' death on a cross says that we're all going to make it to heaven anyway."

Impostor #3: *The Do Your Best to Fit Me into Your Schedule Jesus*

"Certainly Jesus must be pleased with your occasional prayer, Bible study and church attendance. Billions of people never engage in those kind of spiritual exercises, so he must be turning cartwheels that you at least find some time for that. After all, with the stress of living in today's fast-paced society and keeping your job intact, your family happy and your bank account positive, the opportunities for those extra reps of spirituality just aren't there like they were when you were younger. Aren't you glad Jesus understands the rigorous demands of life and doesn't expect that much from you?"

Impostor #4: *The Hey, No Big Deal, Mellow Out a Minute Jesus*

"You saw the movie, didn't you? Wasn't Jesus cool? Absolutely nothing bothered him. He even told those guys who nailed him to the cross that they were going to be forgiven. And I know you haven't been that bad! My guess is had Jesus been living in the 1960s, he would have owned a Volkswagen van, showed up at Woodstock and hung out with the hippies. He was always real low-key, wore the same clothes every day, went to the biggest parties, made tubs of wine at dragging wedding receptions and even took naps in the middle of the day. Now isn't that your type of Messiah?"

Impostor #5: *The Follow Me and Your Financial Future Is Secure Jesus*

"Did you know that if you commit your life to Jesus you'll greatly increase your business prospects? Just give him a little of your time and you might be holding the winning lottery ticket real soon. Tithe your part-time paycheck and the CEO position you've dreamed of is right around the corner. You know the promise—ask for anything and it will be given to you! There's absolutely no way that Jesus would want you to be poor, or even middle class. Think about it—if you were to make a million, how many good things could you do with that kind of money?"

Impostor #6: *The Won't You Be My Neighbor Jesus*

"Did you know that Jesus was a lot like Mr. Rogers? He was sensitive all the time, donning the sweater for a softer touch and ready to appeal to our childlike hearts on a regular basis. Jesus was as popular with the adults of his day as Fred was with the kids in his. No kidding—you can mess up big time all the time and still be his neighbor any time."

Impostor #7: *The All Your Problems Will Go Away If You Follow Me Jesus*

"Could this be the reason your marriage has been a bit rocky lately? No wonder your kids haven't been obeying you. Now you can understand why you didn't get that promotion. Just a little more commitment to Jesus and you should be problem free before long."

These first seven impostors are all quite attractive. Most of us would have few problems devoting our lives to any of these so-called Saviors. We would be frantically searching for a pen and eager to sign on the contract's dotted line because they all have a seductive appeal to our selfish natures.

Now that we've considered the more enticing Messiah types, let's discuss some models of Jesus on display that won't have many people standing in line to take a peek. None of these will win any popularity contests, nor will they do well on any public approval polls. And they are equally devastating. The first seven impostors lead people to a false sense of security in regard to their standing with God. These last five can cause people to hate the head coach, so trying out for the team or finishing the season aren't likely to happen.

Impostor #8: *The Don't Bother Trying Because You Won't Be Able to Make It Jesus*

"Who could really do all that religious stuff anyway? According to Jesus, you're frequently committing adultery with just a little lust, and you're murdering your fellow man on the freeway with your look of disgust concerning his horrific driving skills. I think that's somewhere in the Sermon on Mount Everest! Even if you did decide to stop sinning, how long would that last? Who's going to help you? The only people you know are the spiritually blind, and didn't Jesus tell a pit parable about that? And what about Peter and Judas? They spent three years with Jesus and look what happened to them—Judas hangs up his Christianity by hanging himself and Peter can't even get the guts to witness to a young girl. And you think you can do it? I think you just need to go your own way and roll the dice in regard to judgment day.

Impostor #9: *The I Can Walk on Water but Can't Keep Your Life from Sinking Jesus*

"Isn't the power of God more of a show to keep you in line rather than proof that when you're in trouble he'll throw you a line? And if Jesus is so powerful, why do you only attend weddings and never star in one? And why did your divorce happen? Jesus can't really help anybody with marriage issues because he was never married. And sure, Jesus did okay with other people's kids, but he never had any of his own."

Impostor #10: *The I Never Have Time to Have a Good Time Jesus*

"Self-denial. Cross bearing. Coming in last. Giving up your seat. Praying in closets. Renouncing recognition. Turning the other cheek. No place to lay your head. Have you heard enough yet? No wonder Jesus always looked so unhappy. He was always serious, rarely smiled and often appeared stern and seriously disappointed with the people he met. Did all work and no play make Jesus a dull boy? I thought you said you were looking for a schedule full of excitement and adventure. Looking at Jesus, I'm certain that won't be happening if you follow him."

Impostor #11: *The Leave Me Alone, I'm Talking to God Jesus*

"Wasn't Jesus a little too lofty to bother with us low-lifes? He was probably carrying an attitude from having to leave heaven in the first place. From what I can tell, either he was in prayer, in a Bible study, in deep thought, in a synagogue, in an extended spiritual conversation or in meditation on a mountain. What in the world would he want with you anyway?"

Impostor #12: *The Let Me Get These Thirty-three Years Over and Get Back to Heaven Jesus*

"Jesus didn't really want to be here. Didn't he do that become-a-human thing out of duty? Didn't he die because he had to? Surely he would have gathered a much larger gallery if he were in love with the human race. And if he didn't really care for the people he could see and touch, chances are pretty slim that two-thousand years later you have much hope of getting his attention now that he's back in heaven."

Perhaps you're walking hand-in-hand right now with one of those first seven impostors. Never mind how secure it feels. Read the rest of the book and see if you should announce a breakup.

Maybe you met Prince Uncharming (impostors 8-12) at an early age and you've had no interest in jumping on his white horse to be rescued from your oppressors. Read the rest of the story and then decide if the one in the saddle is different than you thought. Maybe he knows where that "life to the full" castle is located after all.

In the case of The Great Impostor, had the victims spent just a little more time looking into Fred Demara's background and credentials, all fooling would have failed. It's absolutely no different in the spiritual realm.

So let's take a quick trip through the Gospels, watch the real Jesus in action and hear what he has to say. Perhaps this will help us to say "no way" to any and all Satanic sales-pitches. Let's contact the Better Bible Bureau and help put these impostors out of business and behind bars where they belong. The prosecution (me) would now like to present its opening statement (a few verses) and commence the trial of these hoaxes from hell.

Let's consider these exact words that Jesus shares about Impostor #1, The Believe What You Want to Believe About Me Just as Long as You Believe Jesus.

I am the Way and the Truth and the Life. No one comes to the Father except through me (**John 14:6**).

Moreover, the Father judges no one, but has entrusted all judgment to the Son, that all may honor the Son just as they honor the Father. He who does not honor the Son does not honor the Father, who sent him (**John 5:22-23**).

Now let's hear what heaven's one and only census taker has to say about Impostor #2, The Everyone Is Going to Heaven Anyway Jesus.

Not everyone who says to me, "Lord, Lord," will enter the kingdom of heaven, but only he who does the will of my Father who is in heaven. Many will say to me on that day, "Lord, Lord, did we not prophesy in your name, and in your name drive out demons and perform many miracles?" Then I will tell them plainly, "I never knew you. Away from me you evildoers" (**Matthew 7:21-23**).

Make every effort to enter through the narrow door, because many, I tell you, will try to enter and will not be able to. Once the owner of the house gets up and closes the door, you will stand outside knocking and pleading, "Sir, open the door for us." But he will answer, "I don't know you or where you come from." Then you will say, "We ate and drank with you, and you taught in our streets." But he will reply, "I don't know you or where you come from. Away from me you evildoers" (**Luke 13:24-27**).

The Lord made sure he worked some time into his schedule to warn us about Impostor #3, The Do Your Best to Fit Me into Your Schedule Jesus.

He said to another man, "Follow me." But the man replied, "Lord, first let me go and bury my father." Jesus said to him, "Let the dead bury their own dead, but you go and proclaim the kingdom of God" (**Luke 9:59-60**).

A certain man was preparing a great banquet and invited many guests. At the time of the banquet he sent his servants to tell those who had been invited, "Come, for everything is ready." But they all alike began to make excuses. The first said, "I have just bought a field, and I must go see it. Please excuse me." Another said, "I have just bought five yoke of oxen, and I'm on my way to try them out. Please excuse me." Still another said, "I just got married, so I can't come." The servant came back and reported this to his master. Then the owner of the house became angry and ordered his servant, "Go out quickly into the streets and alleys of the town and bring in the crippled, the blind and the lame. "Sir," the servant said, "What you ordered has been done, but there is still room." Then the master told his servant, "Go out to the roads and country lanes and make them come in, so that my house will be full. I tell you, not one of those men who were invited will get a taste of my banquet" (**Luke 14:16-24**).

Here are a few "big deal" statements concerning Impostor #4,

The Hey, No Big Deal, Mellow Out a Minute Jesus:

And if anyone causes one of these little ones who believe in me to sin, it would be better for him to be thrown into the sea with a large millstone tied around his neck. If your hand causes you to sin, cut it off. It is better for you to enter life maimed than with two hands to go into hell where the fire never goes out (**Mark 9:42-44**).

Anyone who breaks one of the least of these commandments and teaches others to do the same will be called least in the kingdom of heaven, but whoever practices and teaches these commands will be called great in the kingdom of heaven. For I tell you that unless your righteousness surpasses that of the Pharisees and the teachers of the Law, you will certainly not enter the kingdom of heaven (**Matthew 5:19-20**).

Now we'll cash in on a golden opportunity to expose Impostor #5, The Follow Me and Your Financial Future Is Secure Jesus.

Do not store up for yourselves treasure on earth, where moth and rust destroy and where thieves break in and steal. But store up for yourselves treasure in heaven where moth and rust do not destroy, and where thieves do not break in and steal. For where your treasure is, there your heart will be also (**Matthew 6:19-21**).

No servant can serve two masters. Either he will hate the one and love the other, or he will be devoted to the one and despise the other. You cannot serve both God and money (**Luke 16:13**).

Let's watch the biblical Jesus as he drops by for a few visits with Impostor #6, The Won't You Be My Neighbor Jesus.

From this time many of his disciples turned back and no longer followed him. "You do not want to leave too, do you?" Jesus asked the twelve (**John 6:66-67**).

Jesus said to them, "If God were your father, you would love me, for I came from God and now am here. I have not come on my own, but he sent me. Why is my language not clear to you? Because you are unable to hear what I say. You belong to your father, the devil, and you want to carry out your father's desire" (**John 8:42-44**).

The real Jesus made sure we wouldn't have any problem discovering the deceit in Impostor #7, The All Your Problems Will Go Away If You Follow Me Jesus.

I have told you these things, so that in me you may have peace. In this world you will have trouble. But take heart! I have overcome the world (**John 16:33**).

Remember the words I spoke to you. No servant is greater than his master. If they persecuted me, they will persecute you also. If they obeyed my teaching, they will obey yours also (**John 15:22**).

Your efforts will be fully rewarded if you ignore Impostor #8, The Don't Bother Trying Because You Won't Be Able to Make It Jesus.

Come to me, all you who are weary and burdened, and I will give you rest. Take my yoke upon you and learn from me, for I am gentle and humble in heart, and you will find rest for your souls. For my yoke is easy and my burden is light (**Matthew 11:28-30**).

The disciples were even more amazed, and said to each other, "Who then can be saved?" Jesus looked at them and said, "With man this is impossible, but not with God; all things are possible with God" (**Mark 10:26-27**).

How about you dry off from the effects of Impostor #9, The I Can Walk on Water but Can't Keep Your Life from Sinking Jesus. Here are a few fluffy towels.

Believe me when I say that I am in the Father and the Father is in me; or at least believe on the evidence of the miracles themselves. I tell you the truth, anyone who has faith in me will do greater things than these, because I am going to the Father. And I will do whatever you ask in my name, so that the Son may bring glory to the Father. You may ask me for anything in my name, and I will do it (**John 14:11-14**).

Jesus replied, "I tell you the truth, if you have faith and do not doubt, not only can you do what was done to the fig tree, but you can also say to this mountain, 'Go throw yourself into the sea,' and it will be done. If you believe, you will receive whatever you ask for in prayer" (**Matthew 21:21-22**).

We'll have a blast as we examine evidence against Impostor #10, The I Never Have Time to Have a Good Time Jesus.

Then because so many people were coming and going that they did not even have a chance to eat, he said to them, "Come with me by yourselves to a quiet place and get some rest." So they went away by themselves in a boat to a solitary place (**Mark 6:31-32**).

On the third day, a wedding took place at Cana in Galilee. Jesus' mother was there, and Jesus had also been invited to the wedding (**John 2:1-2**).

I have come that they may have life, and have it to the full (**John 10:10**).

I definitely think it's time to interrupt Impostor #11, The Leave Me Alone, I'm Talking to God Jesus.

Jesus entered Jericho and was passing through. A man was there by the name of Zacchaeus; he was a chief tax collector and was wealthy. He wanted to see who Jesus was, but being a short man he could not, because of the crowd. So he ran ahead and climbed a sycamore fig tree to see him, since Jesus was coming that way. When Jesus reached the spot, he looked up and said to him, "Zacchaeus, come down immediately. I must stay at your house today." So he came down at once and welcomed him gladly (**Luke 19:1-6**).

People were bringing little children to Jesus to have him touch them, but the disciples rebuked them. When Jesus saw this, he was indignant. He said to them, "Let the little children come to me, and do not hinder them, for the kingdom of God belongs to such as these. I tell you the truth, anyone who will not receive the kingdom of God like a little child will never enter it." And he took the children in his arms, put his hands on them and blessed them (**Mark 10:13-16**).

Let's get to the evidence as fast as we can and expose Impostor #12, The Let Me Get These Thirty-three Years Over and Get Back to Heaven Jesus.

I am the good shepherd; I know my sheep and my sheep know me—just as the Father knows me and I know the Father—and I lay down my life for the sheep. I have other sheep that are not of this sheep pen. I must bring them also. They too will listen to my voice, and there shall be one flock and one shepherd. The reason my Father loves me is that I lay down my life—only to take it up again. No one takes it from me, but I lay it down of my own accord (**John 10:14-18**).

Jerusalem, Jerusalem, you who kill the prophets and stone those sent to you, how often I have longed to gather your children together, as a hen gathers her chicks under her wings, but you were not willing (**Matthew 23:37**).

The prosecution will rest its case for the time being. There will be an abundance of evidence in later chapters to convict these impostors of their heinous crimes against humanity.

Sadly, most people's perception of Jesus is based on a single snapshot and few have bothered to methodically turn through the pages of his entire photo album. At best, most have seen a few pictures of the baby and perhaps a few additional photos of his last days on Earth. But what about the thirty-three years in between?

None of us want to be judged by a single picture, especially when it's not a flattering one. You know, that picture you wish had never been taken. The one that doesn't accurately depict the real you. What if someone judged you by that one photo? Wouldn't you want them to meet the real you a number of times and judge you by those encounters? Of course you would! It's no different for Jesus. My goal in this book is to help you find some of the best pictures of Jesus (actually, they're all amazing). Then and only then will you get *the* picture!

Fred Demara died of a heart attack in 1982 at the age of sixty. He fooled a lot of people in his era as The Great Impostor, then made noble efforts later in his life to bring truth to others. From pretender to preacher, Demara appeared to have taken a significant step in the right direction. But the only question that really mattered upon his death was this: Did the real Great Impostor, Satan, persuade Demara to follow a phony Jesus, and did he accept the offer? And it's the only question that will matter for you and me as well when we leave this world.

All spoke well of him and were amazed at the gracious words that came from his lips. "Isn't this Joseph's son?" they asked.

—Luke 4:22

CHAPTER SIX

Saturday at the Synagogue

Most of the synagogue-goers were familiar with the man scheduled to be one of the speakers that Saturday morning. He had lived there as a boy, and many adults had seen him interact with their children on the streets, in the schools and at the synagogue. Some had watched as he and his father worked tirelessly under the Nazareth sun to build or repair houses. Or they had seen him in their own homes giving an estimate of what it would cost to repair a leaky roof. Business owners knew of him from the times he would come to their stores and buy the family's food for the evening meal or take his father's tools to be sharpened.

"He was a good boy," they said.

They all agreed he never got into trouble like many of the other youngsters, honored his parents to the point of making the other children jealous, and seemed to be a fair, honest and hardworking carpenter-in-training looking to one day take over the family business. He was a positive in the city known mostly for negatives. People had marveled at his regular synagogue attendance, his propensity for memorizing Scripture and his zeal to arouse a lukewarm heart. His baptism in the nearby Jordan River had been deemed a bit unusual with rumors of doves and deep voices, but hey, those were only rumors. A forty-day desert disappearance seemed a little strange, but everything was back to normal for him upon his return.

Many Israelites were holding out hope that he might be the one they had been reading about in their Scriptures around the dinner table and talking about every Saturday at worship for as long as they could remember. John the Baptist was even saying he was the one. And John was a well-respected prophet, despite his lack of clothing savvy and his highly unusual diet of locusts and honey.

"Is this the Son of David?" they cautiously asked one another.

"Is this the Messiah? Is he the fulfillment of Old Testament prophecy? Is this the time for God to rally Israel? And can all this "good" actually happen here in Nazareth?"

That Saturday morning many would be making up their minds. They were pretty open to Jesus being the one, but how would he preach? Would he communicate with as much passion as David did in the Psalms? Would his wisdom be as obvious as Solomon's was to those he instructed?

They were all eagerly anticipating the greatest Saturday their synagogue had every witnessed. This lesson would be sure to stir even the most uncommitted members to action. No doubt everybody would be signing up for the Jesus team after the closing prayer. It was just a matter of what position they would be playing. Being convinced Jesus was truly on a mission from God, they would be the first to enthusiastically jump on the "Jesus Is the Messiah" bandwagon. The stage was set. This was going to be just the beginning of big things in Israel. Everybody could anticipate the Sunday paper's frontpage headline: *"Nazareth Resident Heralded as Savior of Israel."*

Attendance at the synagogue was about double the norm that day. People who hadn't been spotted in weeks managed to drag their "leave me alone, this is the Sabbath" bones out of bed and into the crammed auditorium. The Messiah would be making his inaugural speech as President of Promised Land Recovery. Late arrivers pushed and shoved their way closer to the front, frantically fighting for position and a closer glimpse of the great one.

And there he was—looking very stoic, sitting attentively and listening to the synagogue leader's opening comments, waiting for his chance to read, then remark on a few of the sacred Scriptures.

Then it was his turn. As Jesus began to read, each soul in the synagogue felt as if the words he read were actually a part of him. He was so poised and polished. But in a strange way, it was nothing fancy, almost as though he was trying desperately to draw attention away from himself, unlike others of high rank who regularly appeared on the Saturday program.

When he finished reading and rolled up the Isaiah scroll, nobody said a word for about a minute. They had never heard or seen anything quite like him before, and they were speechless. Soon the silence turned to quiet whispers as compliments started to emerge.

"Best, by far, that I've ever heard."

"Did you hear that voice?"

"He can't stay in the carpentry shop."

"I sure hope he's speaking next week, too."

"My daughter really needs to meet that man."

Others looked at each other but said nothing. They didn't need to speak. They knew what each other was thinking. Thoughts of "this is him, yes this is really him" filled their minds. Then, one by one, they spoke.

"We knew he was going to be something someday."

"I can't wait to shake his hand on the way out, let him know how much I appreciated his words and that I'm definitely coming back."

"I wonder what he will want me to do in his kingdom."

"I can't wait to hear his specific strategy for getting our nation back on top again."

"This is going to be even better than the days of David and the stories we've heard of Solomon's success."

Everybody had something to say. None of it was critical. Yet only minutes later, fury bore its way through the thick synagogue walls and into the hearts of those present that morning. With hatred in their hearts replacing the outpourings of praise from only moments earlier, those listening to Jesus rose from their seats, drove him out of their synagogue and enacted plans to kill him by throwing him down a cliff.

Something in Jesus' final comments threw them down a cliff. It was that "something" about the Gentiles and they just couldn't stomach it. Surely a true Jewish king eager to secure independence from the reigning Roman Empire and bring Jehovah back to the throne wouldn't dare mention Gentiles, let alone highlight them as positive examples.

"Naaman? No way!"

"A widow from Zarephath? Zero chance!"

"How dare he try to challenge us during his first sermon."

"If he were the actual Son of God, he would have allowed us to warm up to his ideas before he tried to challenge our hearts."

"And what about all the good we've done? I didn't hear anything about that."

"How about some applause for each of us for not abandoning our faith in the midst of this unfair Gentile domination?"

"How about cutting us some slack instead of cutting us to the heart?"

"I knew his upbringing was questionable."

"I thought he looked a little glassy-eyed at times."

"My gut about him was right. I should have stuck with my first instinct."

"We should have known a carpenter could never be groomed for such an important political role."

"Hey, Jesus. Go back to your hammer and nails and leave us alone."

Jesus wasn't what they expected that Saturday morning at the synagogue. His message wasn't even close to what they had in mind. To them, his Messianic strategy was stupid, suspect at best. So they missed him. They missed the Messiah. The God who created the universe had been speaking in their synagogue that day, yet somehow they believed it was best to rid the Earth of him.

Jesus said to them, "If God were your Father, you would love me, for I have come from God. I have not come on my own; God sent me. Why is my language not clear to you? Because you are unable to hear what I say."

–John 8:42-43

CHAPTER SEVEN

My Kind of Messiah

C halk it up to preconceptions. Or personal bias. Or prejudice.
Or pride. Whatever it was, it was pathetic. Can you believe it?
They were about to murder the Messiah—and this after just
one message! And the sermon wasn't even that long! And if not for a
heroic Houdini act by Jesus enabling him to slip away from the angry
mob, they would have succeeded (**Luke 4:14-30**).

But before we get too judgmental and pat ourselves on the back
because we would never do such a thing, perhaps the reason we don't
have any problem with Jesus is because we've created a modern-day
Jesus who better fits our lifestyle. Better for our schedule. Better for our
children. Better for our bank account. Maybe we've glanced over some
of those Scriptures that might tempt us to get angry at him or question
his mental capacity, so getting rid of the real Jesus by tossing him down
an imaginary cliff has never even crossed our minds.

Jesus has always been a big problem for anybody looking for their
own kind of Messiah. He's a huge problem for those searching for
the most popular path or the latest line, but not a Lord. Billions have
missed Jesus over the years because he didn't fit. He didn't make sense
initially. In their opinion, he didn't look like, talk like, walk like or live
like a Son of God was supposed to. As a result, many people, both
religious and non-religious, didn't like him.

For most of the religious Jews, Jesus became labeled as a

false prophet, a pain in the neck and a possible disruption to the compromised peace plan they were able to enjoy under Roman rule. To the Gentile unbeliever, Jesus was just another Jew claiming to have the inside scoop on matters pertaining to their Law. No doubt he was a hypocrite like all the others had been, possessing selfish motives, soon to disappear and never be heard from again.

But initially, Jesus fit for many of those in Israel, and his amazing display of miracles was a big boost to their beliefs.

"So, you think Moses had some good credentials? He merely parted the water. Jesus walks on it! Moses only gathered manna. Jesus makes it!

In the first century, Jews longing for the Messiah's arrival were in the ready position, anxiously awaiting the crowning of a new and improved King David. Most believed he would confidently lead their nation to independence from Rome, the stated and hated enemy of Israel who occupied and governed their God-given Promised Land. So at first, many Israelites were ready and willing to follow Jesus. He was destined for greatness in their minds, and it appeared to be only a matter of time until the fight for Israel's freedom had been won.

And based on the miracles Jesus was performing, it looked to be a sure victory for Israel—a permanent food supply, control of the weather to aide them in developing major battle strategies, power to raise the dead and maintain a never-ending supply of soldiers and plenty of wine for the victory celebration.

Then, one by one, they heard him speak—on a hillside, in a neighbor's home, at the synagogue or by the lake—and they discovered his unconventional battle plan. Turning the other cheek? That had to be tongue-in-cheek. Going the second mile for someone? That was at least a mile off-base. Having treasure in heaven as your main focus? What about the here-and-now hopes for treasure on Earth?

At one time, all spoke well of him when they heard him teach. Soon, few had anything good to say about him. At one point in his ministry, thousands were willing to escort him to a conference with the Jewish higher-ups to discuss attack strategy (**John 6:14-15**). But then he started talking like a fool and saying something strange about how his greatest victory would be achieved when he was lifted up on a cross. The problem was simple—most people wanted him as their commander in chief while Jesus talked about being their crucified chief.

Somewhere in our sinful natures, we all want our own type of Messiah. That's why God chooses. We can easily become self-righteous when we analyze the rejection of Jesus by the first-century Jews, but Jesus would have been met with opposition had he come to any group of people at any time in history, Jew or Gentile. Consider some of these possibilities of Jesus coming to America in the past 80 years and announcing himself as the Messiah. Do you think the majority of Americans would have had any problems embracing him?

1940-1950—Half American, half Japanese; last seen preaching at a peace rally promoting the destruction of atomic weapons.

1950-1960—African-American; factory worker; last seen eating at an all-white restaurant and preaching social reform.

1960-1970—Long hair, hippie type; wearing tie-dye T-shirt with humungous peace sign; last seen talking to pot smokers at a rock concert.

1970-1980—Vietnam veteran; unemployed and paralyzed from the waist down; last seen in Washington D.C. preaching about equal opportunity for the disabled.

1980-2005—Middle Eastern descent; mother born in Iran, father from Iraq; distant relative of Saddam Hussein; early years spent in Afghanistan; last seen speaking with Al Qaida soldiers in a mountain cave.

2005-2020—Mexican-American; studying to become a U.S. citizen; working in a California vineyard; last seen speaking to members of a notorious drug cartel.

Perhaps now you can better understand the Jews and their struggle with Jesus. For most, it was due to their worldliness—their physical, emotional and national desires had taken precedence over their willingness to engage in an invisible spiritual war. They were more interested in getting ahead than getting God. More interested in finding comfort than finding Christ. More interested in demanding their rights than doing what was right. More interested in politics than people. More interested in dealing with Rome than dealing with their sin.

And there stood Jesus—right in the midst of a nation that was in desperate need of spiritual revival. He had already been introduced by angels and announced by a highly respected prophet as the Son of God. But, alas, he was a carpenter from Nazareth with a questionable beginning.

Strike 1: A questionable beginning

"Is he really a full-blooded Jew? How can we be sure that Joseph actually was his father? Maybe he's a half-breed—a Samaritan! The real Messiah would never leave those questions unanswered."

Strike 2: A carpenter

"But he's working class. Blue collar. Uneducated. How could he possible know how to develop successful plans to deal with Rome? And even if he did, could someone from that background lead our nation to long-term peace and financial prosperity?"

Strike 3: Nazareth

"A Messiah from Nazareth? Not in a million years! That's the city of low-lifes. No past leader of any significance has come from within twenty miles of there."

There were many more strikes to add to the list. But for most first-century seekers of the Messiah, these three were more than enough to declare Jesus out! The few who were willing to look beyond those three issues might get hung up on some of these other matters.

"He hangs out a whole lot with losers like tax collectors, drunks and prostitutes" (**Matthew 9:11**).

"He really has nothing that's physically attractive or alluring about him. Who's going to be drawn to him anyway?" (**Isaiah 53:2**).

"Doesn't his own family even think he needs professional help?" (**Mark 3:20-21**).

It really didn't matter what Jesus did or how he did it. Most of his own countrymen weren't going to accept him as their Messiah.

If he preached the most incredible, "I've never heard anything like it before" sermon, they found a loophole (**John 6:32-66**).

If he miraculously healed a lifetime invalid, it was done on the wrong day (**John 5:1-12**).

If he brought back sight to the blind, opponents saw it as the work of the devil (**John 9:13-34**).

Even when Jesus raised Lazarus from the dead and his popularity was becoming widespread, the jealous Jewish leaders believed it to be in the best interest of their nation to end his life (**John 11:45-53**).

At the end of his days, the silent and surrendered Jesus was put to death, and on a cross of all places. To most of the Jews, that was a sure sign he wasn't the Messiah. Certainly if he were the actual Son of God, a heavenly rescue operation would have started long before he found himself in that pitiful predicament (**Matthew 27:41-43**).

And when Jesus walked out of his tomb breathing after three days dead, many Jews quickly discarded the resurrection option and instead accepted the fabricated story of the stolen body (**Matthew 28:11-15**).

For most people, there was absolutely no way. The odds of Jesus being the Messiah were about as good as a Little League baseball team beating the Los Angeles Dodgers.

"Jesus is just not our kind of Messiah."

What kind of Messiah have you possibly created? What is the picture of Jesus you have hanging in the front room of your heart? Does his welcoming spirit toward all types of people bother your biases? Does his message of discipleship disrupt your religious peace? Is his salvation message too narrow-minded for your "all roads lead to heaven" philosophy?

The Bible and its revelation of Jesus will always address our pride and preconceptions. It will do with Jesus in written form what Jesus did to the Jews in human form in the first century—tell us the truth and refuse to change a single thing. We may like what we see. We may not. But until we are willing to completely accept him and his message, we, too, will miss the most amazing man who ever lived.

*When Jesus came to the region of
Caesarea Philippi, he asked his disciples,
"Who do people say the Son of Man is?"*

–Matthew 16:13

CHAPTER EIGHT

The Survey Says

Almost everybody in Israel had an opinion about Jesus, ranging from "Watch out, he's a demon" to "Oh my, he's a deity," and everything else in between. Most in Jerusalem and throughout all Judea had at least heard about him. During his three-year public ministry, thousands had seen Jesus or listened to him preach. Some had talked with him on a casual level, while others were given the chance to have a more lengthy conversation with the controversial man from Nazareth. Everyone who was privileged to be in his presence had seen and heard exactly the same things. There were incredible miracles to convince even the greatest skeptics, tantalizing sermons to amaze even the most educated listeners, unparalleled acts of kindness to soften even the hardest of hearts and astounding claims to arouse even the most uninterested bystanders.

To the general observer, Jesus appeared to be consistent. His messages were always clear and to the point. His kindness was viewed as a constant and without prejudice, and he had nothing on his previous record to indicate that he might be a potential problem. But what would the first-century surveys and public opinion polls have said about Jesus?

Let's take another brief journey though the Gospels and consider what some of the three-million residents of Israel were saying. Some of these opinions were being shared because of faulty information, others because people were giving in to peer pressure. Some were spoken by those who owned a bad heart, some by those who had a believing faith. But one thing was certain—Jesus was the talk of the town.

If God had decided to send Jesus to begin his ministry today, I'm pretty sure a story about him would regularly appear in your local newspaper, and thoughts and opinions coming from those who saw him in person would be posted on all the social media outlets. His latest activities would probably be discussed on the various nightly newscasts. Daytime talk-show hosts would seek to secure him as a guest on their programs, and nighttime hosts would find a way to weave him into their monologues. He would probably be kept under constant surveillance by the local and national authorities, and high-ranking government officials would likely go undercover to gather valuable information about him and his followers, just to make sure Jesus didn't get too far out of hand.

With the onslaught of information about Jesus being circulated around Israel—some of it right, some of it wrong and some of it way out of context—the public had become quite divided on what a proper response to Jesus should be. Should they ignore him or hang on his every word? Should they arrest him or follow him? Should they bury him or believe in him?

Here's a sampling of that information being shared from three different categories of people—the haters, the hopefuls and the heralds.

The Haters

"This fellow is blaspheming" (**Matthew 9:3**).
"Here is a glutton and a drunkard, a friend of tax collectors and sinners" (**Matthew 11:19**).
"That deceiver" (**Matthew 27:63**).
"He is out of his mind" (**Mark 3:20-21**).
"He is possessed by Beelzebub" (**Mark 3:22**).
"By Beelzebub, the prince of demons, he is driving out demons" (**Luke 11:15**).
"Who gave you this authority?" (**Luke 20:2**).
"Who do you think you are?" (**John 8:53**).
"This man is not from God, for he doesn't keep the Sabbath" (**John 9:16**).
"You, a mere man, claim to be God" (**John 10:33**).

The haters all had their reasons. None of them were valid. From blasphemer to bad-company keeper, from deceiver to demon possessed, from crazy to cocky—these were some of the careless and caustic words and phrases being used to describe Jesus. One of those comments even came from members of Jesus' own family, as some of his kin had developed serious concerns about his mental state. But that "out of his mind" reference was simply because they were temporarily out of theirs. Thankfully, that accusation was relatively short-lived, as many of Jesus' own family would later become his disciples. We don't know if any of the other haters ever overcame their blatant disregard for truth and the truth-teller. One thing we do know, however—they were given more than enough time and reasons to change their minds and rescind their statements. And had that happened, and knowing how Jesus dealt with his enemies at every turn, he would have been more than pleased to offer them plenty of mercy and grace.

The Hopefuls

"Could this be the Son of David?" (**Matthew 12:23**).

"John the Baptist, Elijah, Jeremiah or one of the prophets" (**Matthew 16:13-14**).

"Hosanna to the Son of David" (**Matthew 21:9**).

"We have never seen anything like this" (**Mark 2:12**).

"John the Baptist has been raised from the dead" (**Mark 6:14**).

"He is a prophet, like one of the prophets long ago" (**Mark 6:15**).

"Good Teacher" (**Mark 10:17**).

"Rabbi" (**John 1:38**).

"He is a good man" (**John 7:12**).

"How did this man get such learning without having studied?" (**John 7:15**).

"No one ever spoke the way this man does" (**John 7:46**).

These were some of the sentiments about Jesus coming from those "waiting in the wings." Each group or individual who shared them had very strong evidence staring them in the face that should have moved them confidently over to the "Jesus is Messiah" side. But the Scriptures don't give us much information about whether or not the individuals making those remarks ever ended up crossing that controversial and dangerous line. But the passion and preaching of Jesus, along with his miracles, his wisdom and the way he cared for people, were at least providing them with the best opportunity to make an educated choice.

The Heralds

"Lord" (**Luke 5:8**).
"You are the Christ, the Son of the Living God" (**Matthew 16:15-16**).
"Surely he was the Son of God" (**Matthew 27:54**).
"You are the Son of God" (**Mark 3:11**).
"Look, the Lamb of God who takes away the sins of the world" (**John 1:29**).
"You are the King of Israel" (**John 1:49**).
"My Lord and my God" (**John 20:28**).

Glorious truths indeed! Two were delivered by Peter, a fisherman and faithful follower of Jesus who had a haul of fish and hordes of fish and bread as absolute proof (**Luke 5:1-11, Matthew 14:13-21**). Another was humbly uttered by a Roman centurion while witnessing the crucifixion drama (**Matthew 27:54**). One was loudly declared by demons from hell as they were being exorcised (**Mark 3:11**). Another was revealed by John the Baptist, a relative and fellow prophet, after a special baptism and an unusual "dove on deity" sighting (**John 1:29**). One came from the tongue of Nathanael, a mesmerized apostle-in-the-making after hearing a most unbelievable revelation (**John 1:49**). Another was confidently proclaimed by Thomas, a doubter turned definite believer upon touching a resurrected body (**John 20:28**).

And what about you? Who do you say he is?

Jesus answered, "Even if I testify on my own behalf, my testimony is valid, for I know where I came from and where I am going. But you have no idea where I came from or where I am going."

—John 8:14

CHAPTER NINE

The Savior Says

While it is interesting to consider the many opinions that were formulating about Jesus back then, only one opinion really matters. What did Jesus say about himself? Who did he claim to be? Was he vague and confusing about his identity, or was he very clear?

As you read through the Gospels, it becomes apparent that most people weren't confused at all with Jesus' claims. Rather they were outraged. His messages weren't cryptic, nor did they need to be deciphered by linguistic scholars to discover the real meaning. There was no hidden agenda. There was no secret code that only computer geeks could uncover two-thousand years later. He never wore Clark Kent glasses. He claimed to be Superman, acted like Superman and was Superman. He made no apologies for being the Scripture-fulfiller, the Savior and the Son of God. He humbly spoke of his eternal nature and that every individual's eternal placement was dependent upon his final decision.

So let's get to the source and examine some of the ways Jesus referred to himself during his days on Earth.

"The Son of Man" (**Matthew 8:20**).

Though Jesus often heralded his rightful claim to deity, he never steered away from talking about his humanity as well. The title Son of Man was the one Jesus used most often when referring to himself. Though he was the fullness of deity in bodily form, he was also called to serve as God's human representative, acting on behalf of others. It was a title borrowed from references to Daniel and Ezekiel in the Old Testament, and one that many in Israel had attached to the coming Messiah. Now Jesus was claiming to actually be that Messiah, the one Daniel saw in his vision of a coming deliverer to Israel (**Daniel 7:9-14**). It was a fairly safe title for Jesus to use in the early days of his ministry, as it emphasized his complete union with mankind. The strategy would also allow additional time for people to warm up to the more radical truth of Jesus being the Son of God.

"The Son of Man will send out his angels" (**Matthew 13:41**).

Jesus is the master of the heavenly beings. He is the creator, coordinator and conductor of the angelic choir, those who minute by minute sing to promote his praise. When Jesus calls, angels answer. When he speaks, they listen. When he commands, they obey. When he stands, they bow. When he sits, they worship.

"I will build my church" (**Matthew 16:18**).

Jesus never said he was the lead minister of the church. He most certainly wasn't a mere member of the church, and he never claimed to be one of the founding fathers of the church. He was the architect, builder and sole proprietor of the one and only church.

Starting the church was decided only by his will and timing. Doctrine in the church was determined only by his binding words. Past and present members of the church were added to the roster only by his approval. And the enormous welcome sign on the front door of his church will be forever removed upon his return.

"The King of the Jews" (**Matthew 27:11**).

Jesus said that he was *the* king, not just *a* king. He was the perfect composite of the greatest leaders from Israel's past, those they respected the most. Jesus possessed David's heart, only much softer. He had Solomon's wisdom, only in far greater amounts. He displayed Asa's conviction, only much more thorough. He walked with Jehu's zeal, only more refined. He showed the concern of Joash, only more urgent. He had Hezekiah's resolve, only for an entire lifetime. He led with Josiah's firmness, but with far greater approachability.

If you took all the best qualities of Israel's greatest kings and wove them together into one amazing king, Jesus would dwarf that king in greatness as a whale would a guppy.

"All authority in heaven and on earth has been given to me" (**Matthew 28:18**).

If angels were given a help-a-human assignment, marching orders went through his office. If the street of gold was in need of polishing, he approved the budget. If Satan wanted a temporary visitor's pass, he would need an interview with him. If any angels succumbed to Satan's tactics, he was there to announce expulsion. If any human sought entrance through the pearly gates, he was the one and only security guard posted at the gate demanding proper identification.

Still today, nobody's heart is softened or opened without a prior search by Jesus for pure motives. Nobody can receive the blood he spilled on the cross unless they follow his specific instructions for a transfusion. And nobody can remain in his school of discipleship without receiving satisfactory remarks on his regular reviews.

He is truly the Branch—the executive branch, legislative branch and judicial branch. He is President, Speaker of the House and Chief Justice of the Supreme Court.

"The Son of God" (**Luke 22:70**).

Most of the Jews had trouble with this title because they knew exactly what it meant. Jesus was stating that he was on equal footing with God, boldly claiming he was the exact representation of God in the form of flesh and blood (**Hebrews 1:3**).

"We've never heard anything like that before," critics would argue.

"Hey, Jesus, God is bigger than the universe and you're not even that big for a human."

"How can a mere man and a mighty God ever be equal?"

"Besides, if God ever did visit our planet, he'd be a lot more impressive than you."

Despite the ridicule he received and the difficulty he knew people would have completely wrapping their finite brains around this amazing truth, Jesus never apologized for being who he was.

"The Son gives life to whom he is pleased to give it" (**John 5:21**).

Giving life to whatever and whomever he desired had never been a problem for Jesus. He was an active agent in the creation of the universe (**Colossians 1:16**). He had been knitting babies in wombs for centuries and no life came to be without his planning and performing. The same was true in regard to spiritual life. If he spotted someone with a caring heart, he was pleased to grant that individual eternal privileges and didn't pass his decision by anybody else. When a lifetime criminal on his deathbed asked him for a spot on his kingdom roster, Jesus promised him a place in Paradise without a committee's inquiry as to whether or not the request was sincere.

"The Scriptures testify about me" (**John 5:39**).

All the Israelites had been trained to be somewhat skeptical about anyone making boasts of being the Messiah. They had undoubtedly encountered a few of those wannabes through the ages who had made the radical claim of being the Christ long before Jesus came on the scene. But every one of those phonies came without power, without proof and without a passport stamped by God. Many would come after Jesus and claim to be the one. They would muster up a small but fanatical following and were soon shown to be false (**Acts 5:34-37**).

But Jesus wanted the skeptics to scan their sacred scrolls and start analyzing. He wanted them to go back to Genesis and check out the final king coming from the tribe of Judah (**Genesis 49:8-12**). He wanted them peering into Micah and discovering the born in Bethlehem connection (**Micah 5:2**). He wanted them to check out the Messianic Psalms and see if they didn't fit (**Psalm 22**). He hoped they would spend a little time in Isaiah and notice that an average looking Messiah was par for the course (**Isaiah 53:2**). And he hoped they would stay tuned for more detailed information concerning his upcoming crucifixion between two thieves (**Isaiah 53:12**), his burial in a rich man's tomb (**Isaiah 53:9**) and his miraculous escape from death three days later (**Isaiah 53:11, Psalm 16:8-11**).

"I am the Bread of Life" (**John 6:35**).

In the desert it was manna—the only God-given source of physical sustenance that kept the Israelites alive on their journey to the Promised Land. It was sent from heaven, satisfying to the taste, sufficient for life and supplied daily by God.

Now it was Jesus claiming to be the new and eternal manna—the only source of spiritual sustenance to keep humans alive and able to reach their heavenly home. He, too, came from heaven, was more than satisfying to those who hungered for righteousness, was completely sufficient for spiritual life and, as God in the flesh, made himself available on a daily basis to all who sought him out.

"I am the Light of the World" (**John 8:12**).

The first-century world was full of philosophers, religious zealots and wisdom providers, all doing their best to shed a little light into a world arena full of confusion and darkness. They promoted their latest thoughts and ideas on how to acquire a better life and a deeper understanding of deity. They promised a clearer picture of God and a clearer path to God. But none of their "light lessons" had the capacity to keep people from their dark and sinful ways (**Colossians 2:4**). Their many fine-sounding arguments (**Colossians 2:8**) couldn't release any of their listeners from spiritual bondage, and they certainly couldn't get them into heaven. In a light sense, it was wisdom without much wattage, ideas with little or no illumination and religion with very few rays of sunshine.

Jesus was different. The one who made the sun, the moon and the stars came to Earth with an even brighter message—*"I am the light of the world; whoever follows me will never walk in darkness but will have the light of life."*

If you listened to the teachings of Jesus, the sun had risen. If you obeyed his teachings, it never set.

If you saw his example, the light in the tunnel appeared. If you imitated his example, you were all the way out.

If you heard about his death on a cross, the stars became brighter. If you embraced it and believed it to be the only means for you to be acceptable to God, they fell into the Earth's atmosphere.

Many people throughout the centuries prior to Jesus' arrival had brought some light. Jesus brought himself. Spiritual patriarchs like Noah and Abraham built campfires. Jesus built a bonfire. Good kings of Israel like David and Josiah shined flashlights. Jesus shined floodlights. Powerful prophets like Elijah and Jeremiah flashed lasers. Jesus flashed lightning.

"I am the Gate" (**John 10:7-9**).

Jesus never showed people to the gate. He was the gate. He was the one and only gate with the power to swing himself open to welcome one and all into incredible pastures of joy.

The gate to forgiveness: *"Then neither do I condemn you"* (**John 8:11**).

The gate to peace: *"I have told you these things, so that in me you may have peace"* (**John 16:33**).

The gate to freedom: *"If you hold to my teachings, you are really my disciples. Then you will know the truth, and the truth will set you free"* (**John 8:31-32**).

The gate to confidence: *"I tell you the truth, anyone who has faith in me will do what I have been doing. He will do even greater things than these, because I am going to the Father"* (**John 14:12**).

The gate to God: *"I am the Way, the Truth and the Life. No one comes to the Father except through me"* (**John 14:6**).

The gate to eternity: *"I tell you the truth, today you will be with me in Paradise"* (**Luke 23:43**).

"I am the Good Shepherd" (**John 10:11**).

Israel had experienced their share of bad shepherds through the years. Ezekiel had pinpointed their major problem to be exactly that in his day, but then reminded his fellow Jews that God had something better in mind for the days to come (**Ezekiel 34:1-31**). It was Jesus he had in mind. In Jesus, God had come to the sheep pen to show the world just how sheep were to be treated.

Jesus knew every sheep. And he loved every sheep. Baby sheep frequently found their way into his arms. Sheep without a full compliment of wool were always on his daily rounds. Crippled sheep were made to feel an important part of the flock and seemed to get greater attention than the rest. Older, retired sheep were paraded as heroes in the barnyard, not has-beens. Black sheep were considered special and unique, not strange and unworthy. Healthy and wool-giving sheep were not just one of the flock but a coat for a cold day. Every sheep had a name that was remembered. Every sheep had protection from the elements and the enemy. Every sheep had food to eat, pasture to roam and fence to contain. This was the day-in, day-out description of Jesus and his involvement with people. Every person he met, whether friend or foe, received the royal treatment when they appeared before the shepherd king.

Nobody had ever treated every individual they encountered with absolute respect. Then Jesus came.

Nobody who was in a hurry had ever made every single person they crossed paths with during those busy moments feel like they were of great importance. Then Jesus came.

Nobody had ever made every outcast they touched feel like an insider. Then Jesus came.

Nobody had ever considered every single person they had ever met to be better than they were. Then Jesus came.

Nobody had ever made the sheep feel more important than the shepherd. Then Jesus died.

"I am the Way, and the Truth, and the Life" (**John 14:6**).

Jesus is the Way. He is the right way, the best way and the only way. He is the way of peace, the way of hope and the way of joy.

Jesus is the Truth. He is the amazing truth, the sobering truth and the entire truth. He is the truth that reveals, the truth that convicts and the truths that sets people free.

Jesus is the Life. He is the good life, the true life and the abundant life. He is the life of service, the life of sacrifice and the life of love.

"My Lord and my God" (**John 20:24-29**).

Thomas spoke it. Jesus didn't argue.

These are just a few of the astounding claims Jesus made about himself. Who else in history had ever made such claims? Who else after him would dare to even try? These claims were nothing short of outlandish. But what is even more bizarre is that Jesus believed them, backed them up and made acceptance of them the basis for being his follower.

Who else in the history of mankind has ever come close to being as amazing as Jesus? Putting any past, present or future life on trial would bring about a quick acquittal—not guilty of being the Savior! Jesus was put on trial for thirty-three years. Just one prophecy about him remaining unfulfilled would have made him just another prophet. One sinful and selfish outburst of anger would have made him just another failed attempt at saving mankind. One look of lust at a beautiful woman would have rendered his blood useless. One ounce of deceit would have meant every other word from his mouth could never be trusted. One angry stare or retaliatory remark while being nailed to a cross would have left us looking for another lamb of God. One bone found from his grave would have meant that we all must settle for only what this life has to offer. But none of that happened. Jesus was everything he was cracked up to be—and more!

The preview of the Jesus movie made many people eager to purchase a ticket to opening night. The actual movie didn't disappoint true fans and was way better than they expected. And the raving reviews of the movie written by those who saw the premier haven't changed for the past two-thousand years. And just in case you haven't seen the entire movie yet, it's still playing in believer's hearts and Bibles everywhere.

As Jesus went from there, he saw a man named Matthew sitting at the tax collector's booth. "Follow me," he told him, and Matthew got up and followed him.

–Matthew 9:9

CHAPTER TEN

Tales from the Tax Man

Imagine you had never heard of Jesus before today and you started reading the Gospel accounts. Do you think the picture of Jesus you'd end up developing would be similar to the same one you have in your mind at the moment?

If possible, it would be beneficial to begin your search for Jesus without any preconceived ideas of who he was. Your chance of finding the same Jesus the apostles knew would dramatically improve if you had just arrived in the modern world after being rescued from a remote island where you had lived your entire life, without the possibility of being brainwashed by long-standing traditions or religious biases. But since this better way of being in-the-know isn't possible, you'll need to do your best to forget the Jesus you've been introduced to so far, just in case he's not similar to the one you can read about in the Bible.

For the moment, forget the Sunday school lessons you were taught about Jesus and instead listen carefully to the people who actually spent lots of face-to-face time with him. Allow them to tell you the Jesus story. And "unfriend" the Jesus you would personally like to create for your perfect world, and let God show you the one who emerged from Mary's womb.

Since it appears first in the New Testament, let's begin our search for Jesus with the Gospel of Matthew. As you read his account, you'll discover many inspiring things concerning the life and times of Jesus.

We'll consider three—the prophecies he fulfilled, the parables he told and the power he displayed.

The Prophecies

As a full-blooded Jew, it was Matthew whom God selected to convince his chosen people that Jesus was indeed the one prophets had been pointing toward as the Messiah. As a tax collector, Matthew was trained to be meticulous with details. Now he would use that training to detail crucial information the Israelites needed to accept Jesus as the promised Messiah. As a once greedy and often deceitful collector of revenue, no doubt he was highly efficient in taking full advantage of every opportunity to squeeze some extra cash out of a client. Now, as an author, he would squeeze as much pertinent information as possible into his biography of Jesus.

One of Matthew's goals was centered on proving to the Jews that they owed Jesus the honor of being their Lord. Whether it was the seven-hundred-year-old predictions about a coming king for Israel and the arrival of Immanuel, God with us (**Isaiah 7:14, 9:6-7**), or David's despairing cry of *"My God, my God, why have you forsaken me?"* that would be echoed by a crucified Savior (**Psalm 22:1-2**), Matthew wove a masterpiece of undeniable truth.

Was it mere coincidence that Jesus was born in Bethlehem? Or did Joseph and Mary travel there to register for a census at the exact time Jesus was to be delivered so the first of God's many flawless predictions about his Son could come true (**Micah 5:2**)?

What about those crazy first few years for Jesus and his parents— moving from Nazareth to Bethlehem, from Bethlehem to Egypt, from Egypt to Galilee, then from Galilee back to Nazareth? Did *"Out of Egypt I shall call my Son"* happen due to luck and circumstance? Or had God led the Israelites out of bondage in Egypt and into the Promised Land more than a thousand years prior to that to foreshadow Jesus' return from Egypt to Israel?

What could adequately explain the directions and warnings Jesus gave to both disciples and demons, telling them they were not to reveal his divine identity in the early stages of his ministry? Was this hush-hush strategy a fear of the stage? Or was it a setting of the stage for

Isaiah's prophecy to be fulfilled (**Isaiah 42:1-4**)?

When Jesus rode into Jerusalem on a donkey announcing his right to the throne of Israel, was it just a desperate effort by him to arouse those on Messiah-watch to action? Or was it an actual event that God revealed to Zechariah five-hundred years earlier, sharing specific information about Jesus' humble entrance into the sacred city (**Zechariah 9:9**)?

Was the overturning of tables in the Jerusalem temple an effort by Jesus to stir up some of the Jewish zealots to action, simply so they would follow his lead? Or was it a sign that someone even greater than Jeremiah had arrived on the scene? A little more than six-hundred years before this event, Jeremiah had warned Israel that God was carefully watching their behavior and was none too pleased. Could this "upsetting" event indicate that God was actually there at the temple in Jesus, not just carefully watching his people, but finally doing something in person to challenge and change their ongoing hypocrisy (**Jeremiah 7:1-13**)?

Were the thirty pieces of silver the Jewish ruling council paid Judas for his betrayal of Jesus just another strange coincidence? Or was it another indication that Zechariah had been led by the Holy Spirit to help those in days to come spot the Savior (**Zechariah 11:4-13**)? Could Jesus have cleverly manipulated this situation to make himself more believable?

If Jesus had only fulfilled a few of the prophecies relating to the coming Messiah, then his skeptics could have easily concluded that those events were just a matter of luck, or from simply being in the right place at the right time on a few occasions. But what if the life of Jesus could match up with every last one?

Perhaps the fulfilled prophecy about Jesus that brought the widest grin and most satisfaction to Matthew as he penned its beautiful promise was the one found in **Isaiah 9:1-2**:

> *Land of Zebulun and land of Naphtali. The way to the sea along the Jordan, Galilee of the Gentiles—the people living in darkness have seen a great light; on those living in the land of the shadow of death a light has dawned.*

This one was personal. Matthew, a Galilean himself, had been blind and living in darkness for as long as he could remember. Oh, he could see alright, but then again he couldn't.

He couldn't see that his quest for riches would leave him empty and always wanting more.

He couldn't see that his deep desire for power and position would leave him with mostly shallow relationships.

He couldn't foresee his daily travel companion called Guilty Conscience walking by his side despite the promise he'd been given that there was little or no chance of him ever getting caught when he ripped off a customer.

And most of all, he couldn't see the pit he would end up falling into when he took his eyes off God and fastened them instead on pleasing himself and acquiring the things of the world.

It was cold and dark in his tax collector's pit of despair. His was truly a life that was being lived in the shadow of death. But all of a sudden there was light. Jesus came by his business one day and it had never been brighter. It was a strange first interaction for Matthew. It was as though Jesus was actually interested in him as a person. But then again, maybe all the attention Matthew was receiving from Jesus was simply because Jesus didn't really know what he had been doing the last few years while climbing the corporate ladder of collections. Surely Jesus wasn't aware of the latest woman Matthew had discarded when he (again) came to realize she was there only for his money. And obviously Jesus hadn't seen him at the local inn drowning his loneliness in expensive wines.

While Matthew raced on the world's fast track leading to emptiness and despair, hope came speeding around the corner looking to cut him off and force him to stop before reaching the finish line. Maybe someone finally cared about him. Maybe someone could finally look below the surface and see all his pain. Maybe someone could finally see how much he hated his life but how he had no faith he could live it out any other way.

Then hope put on its brakes, pulled over and made its way behind the booth and into Matthew's heart. Jesus tossed him the rope intertwined with grace and truth and Matthew couldn't believe what he was hearing.

"*Me? You want me? You want me to come to work for you? And you want me to come to work for you now?*"

Matthew accepted the lucrative offer from Jesus, absolutely astounded that he was never asked for a résumé or references.

The Parables

No other Gospel contains as many parables as Matthew's. And who better to relay them to us than him? No doubt he was a master storyteller himself. He had learned to tell many clever ones over the years that sounded so believable, like why someone owed ten denarii in taxes to Rome when it was really only seven. When fellow charlatans gathered back at central headquarters and recalled their latest revenue ripoffs, surely Matthew chimed in with his best deceiving of the day. He loved telling those tales, but none compared to the stories he heard flowing from the mouth of Jesus.

How could an ordinary man make dirt and dead seeds come alive, explaining all of mankind's responses to God in just two paragraphs (**Matthew 13:1-23**)?

How could someone take weeds and wheat and use them to explain judgment day and the patience of God (**Matthew 13:24-30, 36-43**)?

Could an average Joe use illustrations of mustard seeds, yeast and fish and get you all excited about God using your life for something significant (**Matthew 13:31-35, 47-51**)?

Then there were the short stories Jesus told about lost-and-found sheep that would bring tears to people's eyes (**Matthew 18:10-14**). And let's not forget the wonderful parable of the wedding banquet (**Matthew 22:1-14**). In just this one parable, Jesus revealed God's nature, God's patience, God's appeal and God's punishment. Who in history had ever cared so much about people and their eternal destiny that they would bring that much meat out of a wedding reception? Then there were the chilling accounts of talents, ten virgins and trouble ahead for goats, all designed to warn people about the perils of procrastination.

No doubt Matthew loved relaying all of these incredible stories.

But even more than that, he loved telling people about the story-teller—the one who happened by his booth one day, believed in him and turned him from cheater to champion of the greatest cause known to man.

The Power

If the fulfilled prophecies and practical parables still left his readers in spiritual limbo, Matthew believed his recollection of Jesus' miraculous deeds would help his countrymen cross over to the Christ.

Matthew was a front-row observers of the sensational and supernatural. He longed for people to see with their hearts what he had seen with his eyes.

He wanted readers to feel his jaw dropping when the leper went from crusty to crystal clear (**Matthew 4:18-20**).

He hoped they would feel his heart pounding as he saw a ghost approaching on the water, only to realize it was Jesus on an early-morning stroll (**Matthew 14:23-29**).

He tried his best to transfer his readers back to the time when he and his eleven closest friends delivered a never-ending supply of bread and fish to a hungry crowd of thousands without ovens or wagons delivering fresh supplies (**Matthew 14:15-19**).

He prayed that his fellow Jews would feel his insides tingle and his goose pimples appear as he shared the amazing story of how a simple touch of Jesus' hand enabled a young boy's heart to start beating again (**Matthew 12:12-17**).

Matthew remembered the stunned look on the deaf man's face as he heard his first words, then tried his best to convey that miraculous moment of Jesus in written form (**Matthew 17:5-9**).

He remembered the singing and dancing around the bonfires as former paralytics tossed their mats and begging buckets into the flames as a result of the healing hand of Jesus (**Matthew 15:5-17**). Then he did his best to bring those celebration memories to the book that would bear his name.

And Matthew especially wanted his readers to take in the long gasp of breath he took the first moment he laid eyes on Jesus beyond the tomb (**Matthew 28:1-18**).

But perhaps the greatest miracle of all was that of Matthew's conversion and radically changed life. His story documents the unbelievable transformation of a cold-hearted man determined to get rich at the expense of others into a soft-hearted man determined to offer the riches of heaven to others, even at the expense of his own life. This was the miracle of a man going from writing up false reports on people's taxes to documenting truths about the Son of God.

Matthew was well aware that nobody then, or at any point in the future, would come close to matching the words and deeds of Jesus. And through what we have come to know as twenty-eight chapters in this Gospel presentation, Matthew left us a perfectly detailed map to locate the treasure found in knowing and following Jesus.

It's amazing to me that God would choose someone like Matthew—hated by many and for good reason—to share some of the most important truths ever known to man. Nobody who knew Matthew for any length of time would have predicted that! And for that very reason, and if Matthew were spending time with us today, he would look for any opportunity to share Jesus with those who finished at or near the bottom of the "most likely to succeed" competitions. If that sounds anything like you, thank God you just had a chance to hear him speak. And thank Jesus that he's looking to enlist you as well in his school of discipleship, warts and all.

The beginning of the good news about Jesus the Messiah, the Son of God.

—Mark 1:1

CHAPTER ELEVEN

Romans, Lend Me Your Ears

While Matthew left a lasting impression on his conservative Jewish readers, Mark went in search of a different audience. Mark would focus his efforts on reaching those living in and around Rome, the commercial and political center of the first-century world.

What about Jesus could impress these unbelieving Gentiles? And what information would be beneficial in helping the Christians there to share their excitement about Jesus with others? What could Mark include in his compact thesis so the busy-with-loving-the-world Romans would get busy with loving the Lord? How could he possibly turn the minds of young men and women away from the pursuit of a good education and onto the pursuit of a great eternity? How could he inspire the sexually promiscuous to pay more attention to the oracles of God rather than the next orgy? What information could he present to the athletes and soldiers to convince them that Jesus was the ultimate gladiator and that his method of fighting would lead to victory every single time? What could Mark tell the businessmen about Jesus to encourage them to go after spiritual matters more than closing the next deal? What could he write that would be more thrilling to the entertainment-crazed crowds than the latest theatrical presentation or championship chariot race? What could he share with the married man that would inspire him to file for divorce from the false god he currently worshiped instead of the wife he no longer wanted?

Despite the vast majority's refusal to acknowledge Jesus as their king, hundreds of residents in Rome had already made the decision to confess him as Lord. Yet the remaining unbelievers in Rome needed another opportunity, and Mark was all about second chances. He had looked forward to doing something significant for God ever since he had been convinced of his usefulness by the Apostle Paul, despite a lapse in good judgment earlier in his life leading to a sudden departure from the mission field (**Acts 13:3, 15:36-38, 2 Timothy 4:11**).

And why not target Rome? Nobody thought much about the possibility of Rome being a place where the gospel message could spread like wildfire, especially considering the persecution against the Christians that was being promoted there by the political powers-at-be. But then again, nobody thought much of Mark's chances to make a great impact for God after his disappointing self-dismissal from an important ministry assignment. So the man who knew the power of a second chance was inspired to take a shot at the stubborn Romans.

God gave Mark all the ammunition he would need for victory as he waged war against perhaps the most difficult stronghold to dismantle in Satan's domain. Mark chose not to include anything about the birth of Jesus or his appearance at the Jerusalem temple when he was twelve. Because it was when Jesus turned thirty that he started turning up the heat.

"At once . . ."
"Without delay . . ."
"As soon as they left . . ."
"Very early in the morning . . ."

Those introductory clauses would likely captivate Gentiles hearing about Jesus for the first time. Jesus was a man on a mission. He had important business to tend to and nothing would keep him from it. He appeared to have incredible focus and energy to do his job, and the Roman workaholic wouldn't have it any other way.

"Repent . . ."
"Be quiet . . ."
"Be clean . . ."
"See that you don't tell anyone . . ."

More impressive details on Jesus were coming from Mark's pen. After all, Jesus certainly didn't lack confidence. He didn't seem to be afraid to say what needed to be said and he didn't seem to care what people thought about it afterward. Jesus would remind them of Rome's powerful war generals of the past, those courageous warriors who paved the way for their luxurious lifestyle and the ones most responsible for keeping vigilant watch over any nation who might try to take it from them. And many would continue to contemplate Mark's thoughts about the man named Jesus.

"So many gathered . . ."

"A large crowd came to him . . ."

"Many tax collectors and sinners were eating with him . . ."

"A large crowd followed him . . ."

"Because of the crowds . . ."

Now it was getting exciting! Not only did Jesus tell it like it was, but he filled the seats! For many in Rome, anybody who could get a crowd to follow them at least deserved more of their time to find out why. And few would be bothered by the "sinners eating with him" revelation. The Romans were world renowned for both!

Belief in Jesus was growing in the hearts of the men and women who were hearing about Jesus for the first time. Then, a possible snag?

"He is out of his mind . . ."

"He is possessed by Beelzebub . . ."

"He has an evil spirit . . ."

"And they took offense at him . . ."

Mark's revelations about how Jesus encountered opposition in his efforts to spread his beliefs probably wouldn't have been a big deal for most Romans. They dominated the world, and the world didn't like them either. Rome had all the power, and most of the other nations under their ruling thumb were powerless to do anything about it. Rome had all the modern conveniences, and other nations under their rule were embittered about being well past due on the promise to bring their behind-the-times cities up to speed. The Romans were well aware of the jealousy and anger among the many nations that had been assimilated into their regime. So Jesus' lack of popularity with those inside Israel did little to tempt readers in Rome to end their investigation of him. If anything, it aroused their curiosity as to the power this man possessed to stir things up the way he did. And like any good story, it kept them wondering about what might happen next.

"Then the wind died down and it was completely calm . . ."

"They saw the man who had been possessed by the legion of demons, sitting there, dressed and in his right mind . . ."

"Immediately her bleeding stopped . . ."

"Immediately the girl stood up and walked around . . ."

They weren't even a third of the way through the story and thoughts of "I'm thoroughly impressed" were being impressed on their minds. Roman citizens loved to be regularly entertained, and the magic and illusion shows were no doubt sold out on a regular basis. Those who attended these presentations of wizardry knew that the reappearing rabbits and disappearing doves didn't actually happen. But just having the ability to make it look so real was a sign that the performer had some special power granted to him as a gift from one of the many gods worshipped there.

Yet no magician they saw perform had ever succeeded in altering weather patterns! None had ever asked a mental patient to be a volunteer for their act and then proceeded to put them in their right mind. Handkerchiefs had mysteriously vanished, but never internal bleeding or blindness. Master illusionists had been observed escaping from ropes and chains, but never had anybody caught sight of a real corpse waking up and coming out of their coffin.

Much more of the same exciting information on Jesus would follow. Much more would be uncovered about the determination and passion of Jesus. People in Rome would notice the same confidence, the same crowds, the same controversy and the same "come out of nowhere" miraculous abilities. These were the things that probably made the biggest impression on those living in the world capital. But then they came to the end of the story, and it likely didn't make much sense to most readers.

"Why would a man with all that passion and power become a pushover at the prime age of thirty-three?"

"Why did someone with so much confidence to speak in the beginning become so silent in the end?"

"Why would someone who had the support of thousands not rally them to his defense to help him fight his biggest battle?"

"And where are the miracles? Start a storm, Jesus! Change the enemy's demeanor like you did with the demons! Lead them to the sea and out into the deepest waters, then walk away and taunt!"

"For God's sake, Jesus, do something!"

It just wasn't supposed to end this way. Perhaps they missed something crucial during their first reading. So a second look at the life of Jesus was needed to make the unusual ending more palatable.

Everyone who chose that course of action would later fill the pews in the Roman church. For most of them, their conversion to the belief that Jesus was their one and only king came as a result of the incredible way he treated his subjects. So like many of those Romans may have done, let's consider the unique way Jesus treated the people with whom he came in contact.

He gave ordinary fishermen the chance of a lifetime to take the lead in the most extraordinary movement in the history of mankind. *"Come follow me, and I will make you fishers of men"* (**Mark 1:16-18**).

He touched lepers while the rest of the "clean" world refused to come within one-hundred yards of their shadow. *"Filled with compassion, Jesus reached out and touched the man"* (**Mark 1:40-41**).

He cared for and healed paralytics, those who were often considered a burden and better off dead, useful only for begging and beefing up the net worth of their uncaring bosses. *"I tell you, get up, take your mat and go home"* (**Mark 2:1-12**).

He spent quality time with tax collectors, the bad boys of Israel who were hated, despised and avoided by most people. *"While Jesus was having dinner at Levi's house, many tax collectors and 'sinners' were eating with him and his disciples, for there were many who followed him"* (**Mark 2:15**).

He miraculously fed a crowd of thousands after a long day of leading instead of expecting them to fend for themselves—not to mention being part of the clean-up crew when everyone's hunger had been satisfied (**Mark 6:35-43**).

He constantly met the demands of adults, yet also took the time to make toddlers a priority (**Mark 10:13-16**).

He acknowledged and praised a widow for her meager temple

offering, calling her two-coin contribution more important than the combined amount of those who had given a whole lot more (**Mark 12:41-44**).

He refused to retaliate while being mocked, spat upon, beaten, cursed at and crucified, giving even his fiercest enemies an equal opportunity to one day receive the forgiveness his death would offer them (**Mark 14:53-15:39**).

Sure, the teachings of Jesus would still be impressive on their second trip through Mark's account. They were sensible and clear. They could see themselves not only believing the teachings of Jesus, but obeying them. But the clincher for many had to be the way Jesus loved people. This was the truth that moved them from simply being aware of the story to becoming radical followers of the main character.

Jesus revealed the immense value of every human being, regardless of gender, generation or gross income. He insisted that Caesar was no better than his cook and a soldier no more important than a servant. He showed that the weak and worn needed to live in people's hearts and not in their institutions. He taught them that their children were more important than their careers and the widows more important than their wages. He modeled how glory is attained in giving up your rights more than in going to battle. And he reminded them all that the amount of love you give should never be based on the amount you get.

It was Mark who brought Jesus and his message of love to the city of Rome. God knew the impact this man, someone well acquainted with failure, would have upon his audience. If Mark were here today and telling people about Jesus, he would be the disciple most likely looking for those looking for a second chance. He would stand outside an abortion clinic and put his arm around the women who came out weeping. He would set up a meeting with the parole officer to find out which of the recently released prisoners would need some extra help to avoid a return visit. He would be found speaking about hope at drug-rehab centers, hovering outside divorce courts and talking to men and women on death row about a possible home in heaven. And if Mark had some free time and were playing golf in your foursome, he'd be the one most likely to offer you another mulligan so you could break one-hundred.

A man who knew the meaning of a second chance came to Rome with the message of Jesus and his much-welcomed announcement of a second chance. And third. And fourth. And—why don't you fill in the rest!

Many have undertaken to draw up an account of the things that have been fulfilled among us, just as they were handed down to us by those who from the first were eyewitnesses and servants of the word. Therefore, since I myself have carefully investigated everything from the beginning, it seemed good also to me to write an orderly account for you, most excellent Theophilus, so that you may know the certainty of the things you have been taught.

–Luke 1:1-4

CHAPTER TWELVE

Doctor, Doctor, Give Me the News

If you had lived in the first century and needed to hire a good private investigator, the author of this gospel would have been an excellent choice. He wasn't one to waste valuable time, and he would have made sure every piece of data he collected was destined to help him solve your case.

Whether Luke ever meddled in detective work is uncertain. But we do know he was a physician (**Colossians 4:14**). And if you had any significant health challenges, you probably wouldn't have been disappointed seeing him. Like any good doctor, Luke would have wanted to make sure you had access to the greatest of care. He would take a second look to verify his findings. He would drop by your home for a follow-up visit to see if your fever had broken. He would run the test one more time just to make sure he hadn't missed anything or administered it incorrectly.

Luke had likely studied for years to pursue his dream of working in the medical arena. He greatly valued physical life and wanted to do what he could to make people's time on Earth as pain-free and pleasant as possible. Then he discovered Jesus. The Great Physician performed heart surgery on the general physician and Luke would never be the same. Oh, I'm sure he continued to help those who were physically hurting. But Luke had a greater purpose now. As he treated his patients, he no longer only cared that their pain would cease and that comfort would follow. Now he cared that they would become aware of the pain Jesus experienced while he died on a cross and realize that comfort could come from following him.

What an honor it must have been for Luke to communicate Jesus to the Gentile world. He had to be thrilled with the opportunity of gathering facts from those who were eyewitnesses to Jesus' ministry and majesty (**2 Peter 1:16-18**). He was familiar with some of the men and women who had followed Jesus throughout his days on Earth. Now he looked forward to meeting more of them during his days of research that would prepare him to write his Gospel account.

Luke would set out to be more committed to this project than he had been to any project assigned to him during his medical training. He would look into this one life more closely than he had ever looked into the history of one of his patients to properly diagnose a sickness. He could anticipate the skeptics' questions and concerns, because they would probably be many of the same ones he posed to his original teachers of the Christian faith.

Luke knew that the "wisdom seekers" in the Gentile world would need to be convinced through different means than the Jews. They would need more than the fulfilled prophecies about a Messiah figure, and more than just another promise of a better way of life. They would need philosophical proof. Jesus had to make sense. His teachings would have to challenge them, but not be confusing. His messages would have to be meaty, but not too tough. His sermons would have to be interesting, but also highly intelligent. Most of Luke's readers would probably agree on a clear philosophy: "We'll take it slow, but it better flow!"

Luke knew his readers would be constantly comparing Jesus with what they knew about the famous Greek philosophers, both past and present. Luke welcomed the challenge.

With those thoughts in mind, and with the task of introducing Jesus to the Gentile world, the good doctor packed his bags and proceeded on his mission. He would travel throughout Israel, interviewing those who had come in contact with Jesus and were considered his closest disciples.

So what did Luke discover in the interviewing process that added weight to his already convinced position on Jesus? What was it about Jesus that most impressed this intellectual man of his time? Why did his work as a doctor no longer occupy first place in his heart? Why were life-saving remedies now considered silver medals and serving Jesus was the gold?

Luke is the only Gospel writer who records the incident of Jesus when he was twelve, talking to the elders in the Jerusalem temple (**Luke 2:41-52**). Perhaps Luke strongly sensed the need to include this piece of information, knowing a little something about all the favorite philosophers his readers would hold in high regard and how they had all begun their trek to greatness at an early age. So at an age when most boys were talking about girls, Jesus was talking about God. While most twelve-year-old boys were looking for the next available opportunity to play games, Jesus was looking for the nearest teacher of the Torah to engage in Scriptural discussions. The maturity of Jesus and his wisdom beyond his years were causing even the most respected elders of his day to shake their heads in disbelief.

Then it was on to eliminating other possible hang-ups his audience might have. Similar to most philosophy proteges, Jesus had also been announced. Someone already well respected amongst his peers had both predicted and proclaimed the arrival of Jesus. Luke felt compelled to record the ministry of John the Baptist to help eliminate a possible stumbling block of someone like Jesus being worthy to follow without excellent references (**Luke 3:1-18**).

As Luke continued to be fed by the Spirit of God, he anticipated more tough questions from his readers.

"Okay, but is Jesus from good stock, and can you show me proof?"

Luke was eager to share about some of the very best branches from the family tree of Jesus, and none was more solid than King David (**Luke 3:31**). Even the Gentiles had heard about David and admired his many accomplishments. He was a legend, not just to the Jews, but his military prowess and poetic psalms were both known and highly regarded in the Gentile world.

Most Gentiles would continue reading Luke's Gospel beyond this point, but not without searching for more answers to their key questions.

"Was Jesus tough? Could he take a punch? He wasn't a pushover was he?"

Luke provided the answer: *Jesus, full of the Holy Spirit, returned from the Jordan and was led by the Spirit in the desert, where for forty days he was tempted by the devil. He ate nothing during those days, and at the end of them he was hungry* (**Luke 4:1-13**).

"But that's impossible, Luke. No man could live that long in the desert without food, especially under those circumstances where he's needing all his physical strength to resist a powerful enemy."

And through the pen of Luke and the power of the Holy Spirit, God was moving the Gentile world in the exact direction he had intended.

"Okay Luke. So what kind of speaker was Jesus? We've heard some really good ones in our day you know."

Again, Luke obliged: *All spoke well of him and were amazed at the gracious words that came from his lips* (**Luke 4:22**).

"You mean every last one of them, Luke? So what you're telling me is that Jesus had no problem in the pulpit? Okay, keep going. I'm still listening."

Still more questions needed to be addressed:

"Now Luke, every great philosopher had the ability to gather a substantial following. Some of them seemed to leave potential candidates for their schools completely spellbound. What about Jesus?"

Luke gladly responded: *Then Jesus said to Simon, "Don't be afraid; from now on you will catch men." So they pulled their boats up on shore, left everything and followed him* (**Luke 5:1-11**).

"Now Luke, you really mean they left everything? Okay, but did all that attention get to Jesus? You can always spot a truly divine teacher by whether or not they get caught up in all the hysteria or if they're able to escape and keep their lines of communication open with the gods. Sometimes we look for days before finding our favorites."

Luke brought more necessary facts to those still needing more proof: *Yet the news about him spread all the more, so that crowds of people came* to hear him and to be healed of their sickness. But Jesus often withdrew to lonely places and prayed (**Luke 5:15-16**).

"Okay, but could Jesus handle the critics? The best we have ever seen can keep on preaching even when the heckling begins."

Luke put more of their doubts to death with the sword of the Spirit: *Jesus knew what they (the Pharisees) were thinking and asked, "Why are you thinking these things in your hearts? Which is easier to say, 'Your sins are forgiven,' or to say, 'Get up and walk?' But I want you to know that the Son of Man has authority on earth to forgive sins." So he said to the paralyzed man, "I tell you, get up, take your mat and go home." Immediately he stood up in front of them, took what he had been lying on and went home praising God. Everyone was amazed and gave praise to God. They were filled with awe and said, "We have seen remarkable things today"* (**Luke 5:17-26**).

"Okay, so you're telling me that if I keep reading I'll see him silence his critics in more astounding ways? This I have to see!"

Seeds of faith had been planted in the Gentiles' hearts as they continued to read Luke's account of Jesus. And like always, Satan continued his relentless efforts to dig up and destroy every last one of them (**Luke 8:11-12**).

"Okay, but what about bringing big points to the little guy? You need to make those difficult concepts simple and understandable to those with the least amount of education."

Luke stood watch over the hopeful harvest and continued watering: *Jesus answered them, "It is not the healthy who need a doctor, but the sick. I have not come to call the righteous, but sinners to repentance"* (**Luke 5:31**).

"Hey, that's really good Luke. Did you put that doctor stuff in there, or did Jesus really say that? But I'm still listening."

Much progress was being made, but the task of showing off Jesus was far from finished.

"Okay, I need to hear his eloquence. Give me some of Jesus' best poetic points. Let me hear the ebb and flow of this so-called Son of God."

Luke must have been thrilled to share the following sermon highlight from Jesus' files: *Looking at his disciples, he said: "Blessed are you who are poor, for yours is the kingdom of God. Blessed are you who hunger now, for you will be satisfied. Blessed are you who weep now, for you will laugh. Blessed are you when men hate you, when they exclude you and insult you and reject your name as evil, because of the Son of Man. Rejoice in that day and leap for joy, because great is your reward in heaven. For that is how their fathers treated the prophets. But woe to you who are rich, for you have already received your comfort. Woe to you who are well fed now, for you will go hungry. Woe to you who laugh now, for you will mourn and weep. Woe to you when all men speak well of you, for that is how their fathers treated the false prophets"* (**Luke 6:20-26**).

"Okay, Luke. I think I'm really beginning to like this guy!"

The seed was now a growing plant, ready to make an appearance above the soil. Gentile truth-seekers would continue reading Luke's Gospel and find more convincing proof that Jesus was in a class all by himself, and that nobody else in history had even bothered to enroll.

What else about Jesus convinced the Gentiles to drop the philosophy gig and go to work for Jesus?

Maybe it was his "love your enemies" standard for relationships, or his blueprints for a "house built on the rock" (**Luke 6:27-49**).

Maybe it was Jesus' uncompromising willingness to gladly accept any and all outcasts into his inner circle (**Luke 7:36-50**).

Perhaps it was his bright-as-lightning transfiguration and the ensuing conversation he had with a couple of reputable dead men (**Luke 9:28-36**).

Or was it his hardline expectations and his refusal to let potential followers play by their own set of rules (**Luke 9:57-62**)?

Maybe Jesus' inspiring and shocking story of the Good Samaritan tugged at the heartstrings of the social reformers (**Luke 10:25-37**).

Or perhaps the many words Jesus spoke on the dangers of money and greed finally made sense to the rich but run-down business owner (**Luke 12:13-21**).

Maybe some were sold on Jesus when they heard how he cried out to God and refused to become bitter when large numbers of people decided not to answer his call to discipleship (**Luke 19:41-44**).

Perhaps a few farmers who truly loved their sheep finally opened up their hearts to spiritual truths when Jesus told his wonderful, wooly parable (**Luke 15:3-7**).

Maybe a desperate teenage boy who had recently been separated from his father due to a rash of selfish behaviors stumbled upon a copy of Luke's Gospel and read the parable of the prodigal son. Could that story have been the impetus for him to come to his own senses and gain the necessary confidence to take that first step on his journey back home (**Luke 15:11-24**)?

Or was it the transformation of Zacchaeus that gave hope to all those stuck in their trees of total failure (**Luke 19:1-10**)? Could they, too, anticipate an invitation from Jesus to leave their less than secure limbs?

Was *"Father, forgive them, they do not know what they are doing"* a wake-up call to the misguided zealots who had been attacking the name of Jesus (**Luke 23:32-34**)?

Did the grace given to the thief on the cross prove that it wasn't too late for the person who had been told by everybody else that it was (**Luke 23:39-43**)?

Or did the resurrection of Jesus finally convince the majority of hold-outs? They knew the exact location where all the great philosophers had been laid to rest, and none of them had ever pushed up dirt or claimed to even try (**Luke 24:1-7**).

We'll never know for sure what segment of Luke's Gospel made the biggest impact on his individual audiences. But we can be very confident that his vivid portrayal of Jesus was a highly effective tool in the evangelization of the Gentile world. Luke used a powerful combination of his worldly skills and his understanding of Jesus to impress the intellectuals of the first century.

If Luke were to make an appearance today and share his thoughts on Jesus, college professors might be on his list of people to approach. He'd probably be effective leading a Bible study with a group of medical students and resident physicians, helping them to deal righteously with their challenging schedules and humbly in regard to their future wealth and positions of respect. He would set up some time to share his insights at a meeting for members of a high school's Honor Society. He would look for opportunities to discuss truth with Nobel Prize winners, Fortune 500 CEO's, Ivy League graduates and members of Congress. It probably wouldn't be surprising to find him at a presidential debate, in a corporate board meeting of a top theological seminary, in a library's research section or at a local bookstore looking to strike up a conversation with a fellow bookworm. Whoever would end up crossing Luke's path would get a terrific chance to be introduced to the greatest man who ever lived—Jesus.

Many Gentiles in the first century viewed Jesus from Luke's large and smudge-free window, finally seeing clearly the supremacy of this one life compared to all others. Keep your eyes on Jesus and you'll see it, too.

This is the disciple who testifies to these things and who wrote them down. We know that his testimony is true.

—John 21:24

CHAPTER THIRTEEN

Bonus Coverage
from a Best Friend

The fourth and final Gospel is John's written account of Jesus, and it could be called *The Inside Edition.* John was there in a gloom-filled bedroom and watched Jesus revive a dead girl without CPR (**Mark 5:35-43**). He stood on the mount of transfiguration and witnessed the conversation Jesus had with two men who had been dead for hundreds of years, then listened carefully as God told him to listen to the one who had been alive forever (**Mark 9:2-8**). And surely there were other times when John received teaching and individual training from Jesus. It also seems that John was the only apostle who actually witnessed some of the crucifixion ordeal. Whatever John's relationship was compared to the other apostles, one thing was obvious to him—he felt loved by Jesus (**John 13:23, 21:7, 21:20**).

John felt loved when he wanted to unfairly exclude others from his inner circle but Jesus refused to exclude him from his (**Luke 9:49-50**).

He felt loved when his idea of aiming lightning directly at some stubborn Samaritans wasn't followed up immediately by a bolt to his backside (**Luke 9:51-56**).

John felt loved when he wasn't forced to take a demotion after selfishly requesting a special seat of honor next to Jesus (**Mark 10:35-45**).

Maybe it was the foot-washing he received from Jesus that touched his soul and ultimately cleaned out his heart (**John 13:1-17**).

Perhaps the love John felt from Jesus reached its apex when he finally realized his sin was being fastened to his friend on the cross— the friend who had never let him down or treated him unfairly (**John 19:17-30**).

Whatever it was that made John feel loved, and whatever it was that thrust him securely across the Jesus-is-Lord line, all the possibilities come out magnificently in ink through the pages of his Gospel.

Like all those chosen to tell the story of Jesus, it must have been an unbelievable honor for John to write about him. Surely he couldn't wait to show off his friend. John welcomed the chance to clean up the Gnostic garbage being thrown out on the streets and reveal the Jesus of Earth and the Jesus of eternity. After all, he had spent three unbelievable years with the man. He had touched him, talked with him and taken trips with him. Jesus wasn't a ghost or a figment of his imagination, and John jumped at the chance to make Jesus real and relatable. He also looked forward to silencing the "Jesus wasn't anything special" critics by recounting those startling statements like *"I and the Father are one"* and *"If you've seen me, you've seen the Father"* and *"Before Abraham was born, I am."* He relished the opportunity to provide even the youngest Christians with an effective tool for teaching and converting others. His words would be a dagger for the swordless and an "absolute" for those living in the world of "maybe."

John recorded the words of Jesus that became one of the most popular Scriptures of our time: *"For God so loved the world that he gave his one and only Son, that whoever believes in him shall not perish but have eternal life"* (**John 3:16**).

His simple observation of a man in love with the human race became the shortest verse in the entire Bible: *"Jesus wept"* (**John 11:35**).

Without John, we wouldn't have known how Jesus embraced the social scene as we watch him not only attending a wedding but helping to supply the refreshments (**John 2:1-11**). And we wouldn't have met Nicodemus and been briefed on the necessity of being born again

(**John 3:1-21**).

We never would have been introduced to the woman at the well and been able to marvel at how Jesus turned a simple "I'm thirsty" request into a sensational "I'm the Messiah" revelation. Or watched him easily scale the social barriers of his day, caring more about the Samaritan woman's soul than the status quo (**John 4:4-27**).

We wouldn't have heard about the healing of an invalid and a later discussion with him at the temple, proving that Jesus cared a lot more about man's eternal condition than his earthly one (**John 5:1-15**).

In John's Gospel, we get to discover the absolute best method of quieting an angry mob in the rocky recounting of a narrow escape made by a woman who'd been caught in the act of adultery: *"If any of you is without sin, let him be the first to throw a stone at her"* (**John 8:2-11**).

Thanks to John, we get a detailed account of a blind man receiving sight and find out Jesus is a friend and not just a faith healer (**John 9:1-38**).

We see the ever-popular Psalm 23 become flesh as John shares the ultimate mission of Jesus: *"I am the good shepherd. The good shepherd lays down his life for the sheep"* (**John 10:1-18**).

And we learn about Lazarus being brought back from Paradise and called out of his tomb by the resurrection power of Jesus (**John 11:1-44**).

Throughout John's Gospel, we see God doing in Jesus what he had been doing for thousands of years, only this time in the flesh—cleaning up the dirt mankind had accumulated in his walk through life: *After that he poured water into a basin and began to wash his disciples' feet, drying them with the towel that was wrapped around him.* No anger. No accusations. No attitudes. Just a bowl of water, a towel and a message saying, *"There's nothing I won't do for you"* (**John 13:1-5**).

To the faithful Jew who looked forward to the yearly Passover celebration like many of us look forward to Christmas, Jesus was the ultimate Lamb of God (**John 1:29**).

To those whose lives were basic and bland, Jesus changed water to wine and encouraged people to let him help them start living again (**John 2:1-11**).

To the Israelites who hated hypocrisy and were ready to abandon any call to submit to their nation's current religious hierarchy, Jesus cleared the temple and cleared the way for them to stick around until the proper leadership could be installed (**John 2:13-17**).

To the half-breeds of the world who were often treated as half human, Jesus converted a large number of despised Samaritans and convinced them that who their parents were had nothing to do with their value in God's eyes (**John 4:39-42**).

To the bakers who found pride in knowing their job was helping to keep people alive and satisfied, Jesus was the Bread of Life who could do the same for them (**John 6:35-40**).

To those who lived with the guilt of sexual sin, Jesus forgave the adulterous woman and gave them courage to come forward without the risk of flying rocks nearby (**John 8:2-11**).

To those living with unwarranted guilt about a birth defect, Jesus put out a warrant for the Accuser's arrest with this proclamation: *"Neither this man nor his parent sinned, but this happened so that the work of God might be displayed in his life"* (**John 9:1-5**).

To hard working shepherds who guided their flocks to greener pastures with heavy doses of care and commitment, Jesus was the Good Shepherd who painted for them a poignant picture of a God who loved his creation and would commit his life to protecting them from their enemy (**John 10:1-18**).

To vineyard managers whose future crop was dependent upon the vine, Jesus was the true vine supplying them the nutrients for a fruitful spiritual life (**John 15:1-8**).

To those who thought trouble in life meant being in trouble with God, Jesus said, *"In this world you will have trouble."* And in one short sentence, he rescued them from their make-believe doghouses and welcomed them into the house of God (**John 16:33**).

To those who had displayed moments of sinful and embarrassing rage that kept them from any hope of ever removing a bad reputation, Jesus stuck with Peter after Peter stuck it to an enemy's ear, encouraging them to make amends and move on in life (**John 18:10-11**).

Of the four Gospel writers, John was the one who would have been most likely to make an impact on the common man, the blue-collar worker and the good ole' boy. As a fisherman by trade, John knew all about working weird shifts, putting in a hard day's work, long hours with little pay and the feeling of being disrespected by the more sophisticated crowd. If John were making his appeal today, he would probably find great pleasure in studying the Bible with the intellectual crowd, but I think he would feel more comfortable with those he could relate to the most. He might travel to the coasts and look to land a job with an offshore fishing company for a few months of fishing and catching men. He would sympathize with the security guard working the graveyard shift and help him come up with a plan to find enough fellowship to reverse the trend of his weakening faith. He might hop on board with a long-distance truck driver and help him face his struggles with family management and purity. John would be one of the first in the church to recognize and call out favoritism toward the educated and upper class. Then he would preach a sermon to make sure the garbage collector and the grocery bagger knew that God was equally proud of them.

John had lots to say about his friend, Jesus. He knew there was much more to tell about him, but where would he stop? How many more books could he have published? How many libraries would have to be built if he told everything there was to tell about his time with Jesus? But if John's readers couldn't comprehend that Jesus was undeniably unique from what he had written, would anything else convince them?

So there wasn't a need for additional information. John recorded just the right amount of miracles, and plenty of divine love had been displayed in his Gospel. And there was also an abundant selection of wisdom for thirsty students to imbibe. Yes, there was more than enough information to make it obvious that Jesus wasn't simply another messenger of God, but that God himself had done what nobody was thinking could be done—he had made a personal visit to the planet in the person of Jesus Christ.

While they were there, the time came for the baby to be born, and she gave birth to her firstborn, a son. She wrapped him in cloths and placed him in a manger, because there was no room for them in the inn.

–Luke 2:6-7

(The following pages contain some material in the hypothetical realm. Some of my ideas as to what might have occurred in regard to the birth of Jesus and his first few years of life are not part of the New Testament record. Yet I hope you enjoy this chapter of conjecture and imagine along with me what those early events might have been like for him and his family.)

CHAPTER FOURTEEN

The Arrival

It all started in a stable. That busy night in Bethlehem when "No Vacancy" signs hung everywhere, in a delivery room full of dust and hay, a godly young woman brought forth a baby boy destined to be king.

The unpleasant stench of manure lingered throughout the barn as the farm animals had been herded into the stable's warmer and safer quarters for the night. Exhausted from their journey to Bethlehem in compliance to Roman law, and staying up through the night to bring their firstborn into the world, Joseph and Mary still found enough energy to honor the one who had heralded this unusual birth, expressing gratitude to God for the roof over their head and the safe birth of their son.

No relatives were nearby to offer congratulations. No medical personnel made their rounds to ensure mother and child were doing fine. It was just Joseph and Mary, some donkeys and cows, the occasional mouse that scurried across the dirt floor and an infant who had been gently wrapped in swaddling clothes and placed in a spare feeding trough found in the barn's rafters.

The makeshift outer garments kept the baby king plenty warm, and Mary's milk and tender touch kept him satisfied through the night. And though trumpets weren't sounded in recognition of his safe arrival, and though the world remained completely clueless about this miraculous birth, God had finished his personal nine-month project in Mary's womb and was now ready to enact the plan he had drawn up for all eternity.

In the beginning was the Word. And the Word was with God. And the Word was God (**John 1:1-2**).

And the Word became flesh and made his dwelling place among us (**John 1:14**).

Can you believe it? God came to live on the planet he created and his first place of residence was a rickety old barn. His first roommates were animals. His first smell was that of donkey dung. His first bed was a trough. And his first visitors were shepherds from a nearby field.

It's not the most likely of beginnings for a king. Unless you already knew how later on as an adult and in the religious spotlight this king would have absolutely no desire for the better life or the nicest things. Jesus embraced simplicity from breath one and hugged it tightly for thirty-three years. He expected nothing and gave everything (**Philippians 2:5-8**). He had nowhere to lay his head as an adult, so why start now as a baby (**Luke 9:58**).

And why shouldn't shepherds be the first witnesses to God's arrival. It was merely a sign of things to come. Most of the religious leaders at the time of Jesus' birth arrogantly concluded that shepherds, those often unclean, low-life, dead-end field observers, weren't fit for important spiritual matters. Sure enough, Jesus would grow up to associate with tax collectors, prostitutes, drunks and other sinners, those same sorry souls the religious leaders in his day would deem unclean and unfit for salvation. Thirty years after his birth, those same spiritual outcasts were the ones Jesus loved to spend time with and save on a regular basis (**Matthew 9:9-11**). And why shouldn't a humble manger accommodate the king for his first night's sleep? It would be two simple pieces of wood that Jesus would be fastened to on his final day.

After the birth of Jesus, there was a buzz in Bethlehem. A few shepherds had stirred the people there with what they termed angelic adrenaline, convincing hundreds of residents to go and take a look at the baby they had visited a few days earlier. People would come by a small room that Joseph and Mary had finally been able to rent after a large portion of the out-of-town census crowd left for home. It was a palace compared to those first few days of parenthood in the barn, and Mary and Joseph were always kind and welcoming to the curious visitors who happened by.

"So tell us the story of how you got pregnant," many would ask.

"So do you think he really will be the Messiah?"

"What are your plans for getting to Jerusalem so he can start his training?"

"Is it possible that the shepherds had a little too much to drink that night and they were just hallucinating about the angelic choir?"

So many questions. So many possibilities. So much excitement and hope. But the baby-born-to-be-king novelty died down quickly, and people in Bethlehem went back to their regular lives. Back to their normal everyday existence and back to their superficial, religious ways. Back to their sin and shallow relationships. Back to everything the baby they had been visiting would one day promise to release them from when it came his time to preach.

A year or so later, Jesus' family was back in the news as caravans of magi from the east had arrived in Bethlehem. It wasn't often that wise men from distant nations came to their small town. Nobody could even remember the last time anything like that had happened. But now they were there for some reason, and saying something strange about an unusually bright star—and that this child they were visiting would grow up to be a star.

Then life for Joseph and Mary took a sudden and dramatic turn. After Joseph went to sleep one night, God went to work on him, revealing specific plans about a different living arrangement for his family (**Matthew 2:13-15**). Upon awakening from his dream, the young couple immediately began laying out plans to turn the dream into reality. But moving to a neighboring country with not much money would be virtually impossible. Yet they knew they had to go. Joseph's dream had been so abundantly clear, and the message he had heard was a matter of life or death.

"Get up, take the child and his mother and escape to Egypt. Stay there until I

tell you, for Herod is going to search for the child to kill him" (**Matthew 2:13**).

So staying in Bethlehem wasn't an option for Joseph and Mary. They had always honored God's word despite any difficult implications, and it would be no different with this current challenge.

Then Joseph shared an idea. Mary concurred. They determined that God had allowed the wise men's recent visit, in part, to fund their upcoming move to Egypt. So they decided to sell the gold, frankincense and myrrh left by the magi as gifts for their son. There was no time to waste, and the money from the sale was a sufficient amount to make it to Egypt and a little extra for the first few weeks there while Joseph searched for employment.

Joseph and Mary left for Egypt with a pit in their stomach. Little did they realize that many of the little boys Jesus had played with in Bethlehem would be brutally murdered within a few weeks when King Herod unleashed his ferocious wrath, looking to kill his competition. Thankfully, Jesus would narrowly escape the massacre. But that shouldn't be surprising either when you consider how often Jesus, during his three years of public ministry, escaped at just the right time from those looking to end his life before his planned departure on a cross (**Luke 4:28-30, John 7:30**).

Now exiled and, like their ancestors, stuck in Egypt, Joseph and Mary waited for the moment when they could resettle back in more familiar territory. Another deep sleep for Joseph produced the plan.

"Get up, take the child and his mother and go to the land of Israel, for those who are trying to take the child's life are dead" (**Matthew 2:19-20**).

One more dream and Joseph and Mary were finally back in Nazareth (**Matthew 2:21-23**). So much had happened in the time away from their hometown. And if all of that happened in a span of about three years, what additional excitement and drama could they expect from that point forward?

And the child grew and became strong; he was filled with wisdom, and the grace of God was on him.

—Luke 2:40

Then he went down to Nazareth with them and was obedient to them . . . And Jesus grew in wisdom and stature, and in favor with God and man.

—Luke 2:51-52

CHAPTER FIFTEEN

From Three to Thirty

Because there's limited information in the Scriptures documenting the activities of Jesus from age three to thirty, most of us don't spend much time thinking about what might have occurred in his life during those years. So I'm about to change that for us in this chapter. Granted, the following material is based purely on possible and nothing on actual. But if any of these things I share are accurate, perhaps they can help us better understand the incredible truth that often seems difficult to grasp—that while Jesus will never deny he's our boss, he'd also like to be viewed as our big brother (**Hebrews 2:10-12**).

We are aware of one event in the life of Jesus that took place when he was twelve. Luke relates the story of a typical pre-teen boy spending a not-so-typical amount of time in the temple talking to the Jewish elders. But other than that, the growing-up files on Jesus are empty. So let's imagine what might have been for Jesus from three to thirty. Let's try to make him as real and relatable as possible. Let's look at more than a quarter of a century of "ordinary living" that could have helped in preparing Jesus for three years of extraordinary.

Do you think Jesus ever got disciplined? Did he ever forget to do his chores or disobey the direction of his parents?

Did Jesus go to school? If so, was he always able to finish his homework on time, or did daydreaming and procrastination get the best of him on occasion?

Did Jesus ever hear his parents make any of these important reminders?

"Jesus, eat your vegetables. You want to grow up to be big and strong don't you?"

Did that healthy hint become his habit as an adult, giving him the necessary physical stamina to make his way around the hilly terrain of Israel, or up the mountain for another all-night prayer (**Luke 6:12**)?

"Now Jesus, what do you say to the nice lady?"

Maybe he remembered to honor their admonition years later when the widow left her mite in the offering plate and nobody else thought such a measly amount was worthy of recognition (**Luke 21:1-4**).

"Jesus, are you still up? You need to go to sleep right now."

Was this some early training for a disciplined life that later allowed Jesus to rise before the sun and spend quality time with God before the rest of the world rolled out of bed?

"Jesus, you need to be a big boy and take your medicine. I know it tastes awful, but you won't get better unless you drink it."

Perhaps the strategy that worked on him as a child would also work on him as an adult while he agonized in the Garden of Gethsemane, awaiting the hour when he would choose to drink the bitter cup of the cross.

"Now Jesus, be very careful. There are a lot of bad people out there and you can't trust everyone."

Did this life-saving advice serve Jesus well as an adult as he constantly stayed one step ahead of those looking to trap him in his words or kill him before his time?

"Jesus, remember what your father said. Whenever anybody comes over to the house, you need to get up and give them a hug."

Did a leper years later receive the loving touch of Jesus as a result of some of the solid teaching he received at home (**Mark 1:40-42**)? Did tax collectors and prostitutes get a warm welcome from Jesus in his later years thanks in part to his parents' lessons on unconditional love (**Matthew 9:9-12**)?

"Son, always remember you're stronger if you walk away than you are if you fight."

Did this valuable piece of parental wisdom help form some of the key elements in Jesus' first sermon? And did it help him to possess the toughest and reddest cheeks ever known to man? *"Do not resist an evil person. If someone strikes you on the right cheek, turn to him the other also"* (**Matthew 5:39**).

What other growing-up experiences could have contributed to his training in becoming our advocate and absolute best role model (**1 John 2:1-2, Hebrews 4:15**)?

How often did Jesus say grace at the dinner table? And how did Joseph and Mary teach him to take it deeper than a legalistic offering of thanks? When did Jesus first realize that the Provider was much more important than the provision?

What did he do with the other kids his age? Did he ever play follow the leader? If he was picked to lead, did he only act out things he knew the other participants could accomplish because that's how he would be one day as their Lord? Did he prefer to play the game as a follower so he could learn the feeling of facing obstacles with courage?

Did Jesus have any stuffed animals? If so, perhaps his favorites would have been the lion and the lamb. If so, did he realize that in one way he was bound to be both (**Revelation 5:1-14**)? Or did he also understand that in another way the lion was his fiercest foe? Did he ever pretend they were fighting each other and the lamb would always come out on top (**1 Peter 5:8**)?

Did he ever color a picture of a tree or the sun and have a moment of deja vu (**Colossians 1:16**)?

What was it like growing up with all his siblings? We do know that four little brothers and at least two little sisters were a part of his upbringing (**Mark 6:3**). When did Jesus first gain the trust of his parents to babysit for them? Maybe the many opportunities to keep his six siblings from warlike behavior prepared him for similar moments of "break-it-up" with the twelve apostles (**Matthew 20:20-28**).

How much did his brothers and sisters struggle with jealousy and envy when they heard their parents share about Jesus' exciting beginning and his destiny for future success? Did any of them ever believe in Jesus as more than a big brother before his death and resurrection (**John 7:1-5**)?

How much interaction did Jesus have with his cousin, John the Baptist? Did they ever challenge one another in Old Testament trivia? Did they ever argue about who's the most radical? Did they take turns preaching and afterward offer each other input?

Did Joseph and Mary ever take Jesus on a trip to rediscover his roots? Did they go back to Bethlehem and walk through the stable where he had been born? Did Jesus ever get to meet the shepherds who witnessed his first hours of life? Did they ever take time to mourn at the Bethlehem cemetery where small children were buried, those who were murdered as a result of the massacre they missed? Did they reconstruct their hurried trip to Egypt to show Jesus how God had protected them along the way?

When Jesus studied the history of Babylon, when did it occur to him that he had been there? Did he ever participate in any of the debates about who the fourth individual was who showed up in the fiery furnace with Shadrach, Meshach and Abednego (**Daniel 3:19-25**)?

Did Jesus play sports? Was he on any teams? If so, and the weather was bad for one of his games, did he ever calm the storm and dry the field without anyone knowing just so the game could be played? Or perhaps he was the team manager or water boy. No doubt he would have gladly carried the equipment since later in life he would gladly carry his cross.

What kind of student was Jesus? Did he ever know what the test questions would be before they were asked?

Did he get picked on or teased? Did the bullies ever gang up to get him? Did he experience as a child what he would one day encounter with the Sanhedrin? (**Matthew 26:57-68**)?

What did Jesus do when he saw others getting picked on or teased? Did he every befriend a labeled loser much like he did later with the woman at the well (**John 4:4-26**) and the short man in the tree (**Luke 19:1-10**)? Did he ever decide to hang out with the homely looking boy just because nobody else would?

Did Jesus have perfect attendance at school or work? Or were there sick days for the Son of God? Did he have pimples or crooked teeth? Did he have big ears or a high forehead? What kind of accidents did he have? Did he ever break a bone running with his friends or jumping out of a tree? We know there were none broken later in his life when he was fastened to a tree, but what about during the days prior to that (**John 19:31-37**)?

If there were tough times at home when there was little food on the table, did Jesus ever remember a nearby location of gold he had created and go buy food for the family? Was there ever an early fish and bread miracle that led to a special delivery by Jesus to some of the poorer families in town?

Were there other private miracles he performed to bring comfort to people before he went public with them?

Did he ever walk on water when nobody was watching just to have a little fun?

What was Jesus' favorite color? Perhaps it was a tie between green and blue since those were the two he used most in the creation. Or maybe it was dark red because it was the only color that mattered when it came to salvation. Or maybe he refused to have a favorite one, knowing man would way too easily get hung up on things like color.

How many times did Jesus go to Jerusalem for the Passover festival? How many lambs were slain in his presence before he realized he would be the final one?

Did he ever take a job as a fisherman just to make himself more relatable to the four men who would choose to follow him first (**Mark 1:14-20**)?

When Jesus attended funerals, was he tempted to show off too soon?

When he watched a wedding, did he feel saddened that he would never be the center of attention at one? Did he ever have to hear some of these words in regard to his extended term of single living?

"Jesus, when are you planning to tie the knot?"

"Jesus, everyone else in your family is hitched but you."

"Why Jesus, I know the nicest girl . . ."

When did Jesus start helping his father in the carpentry shop? While sweeping up the wood shaves, did he see it as an opportunity to rejoice as he anticipated sweeping away the sins of those who would one day follow him? When his hammer struck a nail, would he ever shake and shiver?

It's fun to think about these things. But only one thing is for sure—Jesus was amazing from three to thirty. He was, at the very least, submissive and obedient to his parents, and that speaks volumes, whether today or two-thousand years ago (**Luke 2:51-52**).

I hope you enjoyed your time on the path of perhaps. But remember, it is only that! If there were other crucial data on Jesus, God would have told us tons about the toddler, the ten-year-old, the teen and the man in his twenties. But all we have is a few days when he was twelve, and we'll have to be content with that. Because for Jesus, life really began at thirty!

When Jesus had finished saying these things, the crowds were amazed at his teachings, because he taught as one with authority, not as their teachers of the Law.

—Matthew 7:28-29

CHAPTER SIXTEEN

No One Ever Spoke Like This

Whether he was delivering words of encouragement to a group of ten, teaching a parable to a gathering of a hundred, announcing a call of discipleship to a thousand or proclaiming a "You're either with me or against me" sermon to ten-thousand, Jesus made an impact on listener's hearts like no other teacher ever had or ever will. And whenever he spoke, one thing was quite predictable—his messages wouldn't be predictable! Sermon after sermon, those in his hearing left shaking their heads in disbelief.

"Did he just say what I thought he said?"

"I wasn't expecting that."

"He's not messing around, is he?"

Even those who hated what Jesus said or refused to accept his words as binding knew that his messages and method of delivery weren't customary compared to others who claimed to channel truth. The lessons given by Jesus were straightforward and always delivered with a seriousness that religious audiences had seldom heard. He spoke with great authority, unlike so many others whose content was diluted with tradition and "try your best" appeals. Most people couldn't remember the last time any teacher had ever held them accountable to upholding the standards presented in the lessons they taught. The

Jews had heard many expositors declare "I think" but very few with the guts to say "I know." They were quite familiar with "You should" but unacquainted with "You must." They were often soothed with "Relax" but rarely spurred on with "Repent." Then along came Jesus!

The Sermon on the Mount, the first recorded message of Jesus to a listening audience, contains the essence of Jesus—who he was, how he lived, what he taught and what he expected from his followers. Similar to every sermon Jesus preached, he displayed an eagerness to make sure his listeners were clear about his standards. He didn't want anyone claiming to be his disciple who had little or no idea about what he taught. And if Jesus were to preach at any church today, he would express the exact same concern.

Many of those who came to hear Jesus that day brought some heavy baggage with them. People had their religious suitcases filled with longstanding traditions and "only tell me what I want to hear" expectations. Their bags were closed and securely locked, never being let out of their sight. Many had been sitting on theirs for years just to make sure they remained closed. Jesus didn't ask anybody to check their bags with him when they entered, but he would expect them to be left behind when they exited.

So what did Jesus say that day that led to such a rousing response from those who heard him? What would bring him from nowhere to be seen in the race of history's greatest heralds to being out in the lead by a full lap?

"Blessed are the poor, for theirs is the kingdom of heaven. Blessed are those who mourn, for they will be comforted. Blessed are the meek, for they will inherit the earth. Blessed are those who hunger and thirst for righteousness, for they will be filled. Blessed are the merciful, for they will be shown mercy. Blessed are those who are pure in heart, for they will see God. Blessed are those who are persecuted because of righteousness, for theirs is the kingdom of heaven. Blessed are you when people insult you, persecute you and falsely say all kinds of evil against you because of me. Rejoice and be glad, because great is your reward in heaven, for in the same way they persecuted the prophets who were before you" (**Matthew 5:3-12**).

In baseball lingo, this would be a leadoff homerun. In football, it's an 80-yard bomb for a touchdown on the first play. Jesus' opening remarks were all about possessing the right heart and displaying the right actions. Be humble. Be soft-hearted. Be gentle. Be godly. Be merciful. Be pure. Be peaceful. Be patient. Be positive. Be faithful. Be happy. These opening lines launched an all-out attack on the spiritual forces of evil. Jesus came with an amazing message of hope that shook the foundations of the world in his day. And it has had the same force in every generation since. Whether it was Gandhi trying to gain independence for the people of India, or Martin Luther King Jr. trying to teach a nation about the evils or racism, if someone taught it "The Jesus Way," they were moving in the right direction. If they lived out "The Jesus Way," they had arrived.

"You are the salt of the earth. But if the salt loses it saltiness, how can it be made salty again? It is no longer good for anything, except to be thrown out and trampled by men. You are the light of the world. A city on a hill cannot be hidden. Neither do people light a lamp and put it under a bowl. Instead they put it on its stand, and it gives light to everyone in the house. In the same way, let your light shine before men, so that they may see your good deeds and praise your Father in heaven" (**Matthew 5:13-16**).

Jesus never intended for his message to stand still. And he never preached a sermon just to preach a sermon because that was his job. He expected his words to be heard, then followed. He refused to allow his listeners to feel good about merely attending one of his lectures and complementing him about how great it was on their way out. His message was always "hear it, believe it, do it."

It's a real tendency for religious people to pat themselves on the back just because they come to church and sit through a sermon, even though being obedient to what they're hearing isn't at the core of their considerations (**James 1:22-25**). That can certainly be my tendency, and I'm pretty sure you've struggled at times with that as well. Unfortunately, many ministers today are hesitant to deal head-on with this sinful practice. Not Jesus. His message was from God, and hearing it without obeying it did not sit well with him. It wasn't enough for Jesus that people knew his messages were salt. He fully expected his followers to tip themselves upside down and start shaking. It wasn't enough for Jesus that people knew his messages were light. He challenged everyone in his audience to turn on their flashlights and start walking.

Today, Jesus' expectations are still the same. If you hear a truth Jesus presents about marriage, you'll need to take it to heart and live it out at home, pouring as much salt on your spouse as possible. If the couple across the street opens their door for friendship, it shouldn't be long before they see your salty marriage and invite you to pour some of yours on them.

If Jesus reveals a truth involving the proper attitude to carry into the workplace, you'll be expected to grab your flashlight every morning as you head off to another busy day in the dark crevasses of capitalism. If your boss is harsh and hardheaded, you'll need to do all you're asked to do with a smile on your face, all the while shining your flashlight in his. If coworkers are bad-mouthing the new manager and look to you for agreement, your silence or your humble call to stop the slander will provide excellent light for the surrounding darkness. With every showing up to work on time, light is present. With every following of specific directions, the light shines brighter. With every kind word and sincere gesture to the boss or a fellow employee, the light becomes blinding.

If Jesus proclaims the plan of God concerning the correct way to walk on your campus, live in your neighborhood or conduct your dating relationship, he expects you to take it from the pew to the public arena.

"For I tell you that unless your righteousness surpasses that of the Pharisees and the teachers of the Law, you will certainly not enter the kingdom of heaven" (**Matthew 5:20**).

"But I tell you that anyone who is angry with his brother will be subject to judgment" (**Matthew 5:22**)

"But I tell you that anyone who looks at a woman lustfully has already committed adultery with her in his heart" (**Matthew 5:28**).

"But I tell you that anyone who divorces his wife, except for marital unfaithfulness, causes her to become an adulteress, and anyone who marries the

divorced woman commits adultery" (**Matthew 5:32**).

"But I tell you, do not resist an evil person. If anyone strikes you on the right cheek, turn to him the other also. And if someone wants to sue you and take your tunic, let him have your cloak as well" (**Matthew 5:39-40**).

"But I tell you, love your enemies and pray for those who persecute you, that you may be sons of your Father in heaven" (**Matthew 5:44**).

Most of Jesus' listeners that day had only heard about lower forms of righteousness. The spiritual bar had been set so low that almost anybody could rise above it. It was simple. Don't strike the first blow. Don't get in bed with the wrong woman. Don't forget to secure the legal documents when you're ready to cancel your wedding vows. Don't feel bad about paybacks because revenge is only fair. Then along came Jesus to schedule everyone for below-the-surface scans to expose the inner heart. Anger is deadly, whether someone dies or not. Lust is horrible, whether your spouse or the attractive person on the street knows you're doing it or not.

So because Jesus cared about people, he spoke out against sins such as anger and lust. He knew the emotional suffering that outbursts of anger caused those on the receiving end. And he couldn't stomach the thought of a woman feeling more like an object of sex than a special creation of God. He knew the value of every human being, and he refused to allow any of that value to be diminished.

Divorce in the minds of many religious people in that day was thought to be a perfectly acceptable alternative to an unhappy marriage (**Matthew 5:31**). The popular philosophy of the day was well known and expedient: *"Just as long as everything is done legally, everything will be lovely. Moses said it, so that must make it right."*

Jesus refused to accept those substandard beliefs and raised the bar on marriage by reintroducing the garden variety and how God had designed it from the beginning (**Matthew 5:32**). God had always intended for marriage to last a lifetime, but in that day, any excuse to move on to the next mate was deemed legitimate. If you didn't like the way your wife performed in bed, you could get yourself a good lawyer and before long get back to looking for a new partner. If she didn't show you the respect you thought you deserved, your fellow man would totally understand your decision to dismiss her from her wifely duties. If her cooking was questionable and dinners weren't "well-done" as you had ordered, you could cancel future dinner reservations with her and go in search of the more culinary kind. If your spouse became debilitated and couldn't do the normal duties of a wife, you could quickly work up a plan to put her out of your plans and into an institution. No wonder Jesus was disgusted with the current trend. And he would be equally disgusted with what he sees today in regard to marriage and divorce. And like a lot of other trends and patterns that were totally wrong, he preached against them and called for drastic changes to be made.

Then it was on to the subject of getting even and biting back. Jesus turned some heads when he sounded off on turning the other cheek and handing over your coat to the one who had already ripped off your robe (**Matthew 5:38-42**).

Jesus really ruffled the feathers of his audience that day when he laid out the expectation of loving your enemies. He riled them up some more when he dared to put the pious Jew in the same category as the pagan tax collector (**Matthew 5:46**). And he had the guts to challenge them to add their greatest foe to their daily prayer list (**Matthew 5:44**).

> *"So when you give to the needy . . ."* (**Mathew 6:2-4**).
> *"And when you pray . . ."* (**Matthew 6:5-15**).
> *"When you fast . . ."* (**Matthew 6:16-18**).

Jesus saw the need in this sermon to remove any and all confusion coming from the popular idea that being religious was equal to being right. For Jesus, that concept was clearly wrong. Where others found contentment in simply performing their religious duties, Jesus found disgust. While others focused primarily on cleaning and polishing their outer selves, Jesus looked to do his scrubbing on the inside. Jesus seemed completely uninterested in recruiting anybody who was content with the current religious standards. Instead, he searched for those seeking change.

Who else but Jesus would have recruited the people he did to be the foundation of a religious movement that would need to rock the world? Who else would pick the prostitute who was too ashamed to pray ahead of the religious man most eloquent in prayer to be the one most likely to move the heart of God to act on their behalf? Who else would pick a pagan with no prior fasting experience ahead of the Pharisee who did it twice a week to be part of his all-important inner circle? Who else would select a tax collector who stole people's money before choosing a proper Jew who tithed his own to join his crew and preach against the evils of materialism?

Only Jesus had the nerve to make all of these weird-to-the-world roster choices. But Jesus didn't care what people thought of his choices. He knew the type of follower he was looking for, and he was completely unimpressed with "spirituality" that was only visible on the surface. While others may have stood in awe of religious appearance, Jesus rapidly removed man's thick layers of piety, pride and public approval and went straight to the heart. What he found there determined his applause.

"Do not store up for yourselves treasure on earth, where moth and rust destroy, and where thieves break in and steal. But store up for yourselves treasure in heaven, where moth and rust do not destroy, and where thieves do not break in and steal. For where your treasure is, there your heart will be also" (**Matthew 6:19-21**).

Seeking after and acquiring material wealth was considered noble in the first century. Many believed that the more a man owned, the more he had been blessed by God. If you had a chariot, you were God's friend. If you owned a second, you were probably a relative. If you owned a home, no doubt you were in God's favor and on your way to heaven. If you also had a vacation getaway, the red carpet would be rolled out on your arrival. Jesus saw it differently.

He refused to equate lots of money with lots of blessings from above, or having plenty of cash with getting personal favors from the Creator. He called his disciples to be easily satisfied, waiting for heaven to reveal their eternal reward rather than roaming the world in a search for earthly treasure.

Jesus had no problem with downsizing. He knew the square

footage of heaven and wasn't impressed at all with the mansions of Earth.

He embraced the simple things of life. He had seen the heavenly banquet spread and was bored with the delicacies of Earth.

He had no issue with giving his money or letting people take his money. He had walked the golden street and sailed the crystal sea and yawned at the notion of saving up for a chariot fit for a Caesar or a sailboat designed for enjoyment on the Sea of Galilee.

The teachings of Jesus contained no information about making lots of money, developing land or constructing bigger and better buildings. He wasn't personally interested in getting rich and he never promised it to any of his followers. Gaining wealth, going to war against Rome or getting back full possession of the Promised Land were never heard in any of his speeches. His desires weren't focused on gaining more property, but saving more people. He expected people to live as though heaven was already theirs and the things of the world never were. He called people to trust and not take up arms. He never owned a home. He never sought political office. And he never held a rally against the evils of the Roman occupation of his homeland.

If his teachings were followed wholeheartedly by those of us living today, wars would be a thing of the past and hunger and homelessness would be eliminated. Young people would long to become teachers and social workers, and every last one of us would consider the thought of getting rich a really bad idea.

"Therefore, I tell you, do not worry about your life, what you will eat or drink; or about your body, what you will wear . . ." (**Matthew 6:25-26**).

"Who of you by worrying can add a single hour to his life?" (**Matthew 6:27**).

"So do not worry, saying, "What shall we eat?" or "What shall we wear?" For the pagans run after all these things, and your heavenly Father knows that you need them. But seek first his kingdom and his righteousness, and all these things will be given to you as well. Therefore do not worry about tomorrow, for tomorrow will worry about itself. Each day has enough trouble of its own" (**Mathew 6:31-34**).

The teachings of Jesus were centered on calm. He encouraged

people to look around at the creation and contemplate (**Matthew 6:26**). He told them to go find a flower and figure it out (**Matthew 6:28**) and to notice a nest and not panic (**Matthew 6:26**). His teachings were about turning people away from the hustle and bustle of life and turning them heavenward instead. His teachings emphasized God's personal involvement in every individual's life and that all would be worked out physically if people chose to work out spiritually (**Matthew 6:33**).

"Do not judge, or you too will be judged. For in the same way you judge others, you will be judged, and with the same measure you use, it will be measured to you. Why do you look at the speck of sawdust in your brother's eye and pay no attention to the plank in your own eye? How can you say to your brother, "Let me take the speck out of your eye," when all the time there is a plank in your own eye? You hypocrite, first take the plank out of your own eye, and then you will see clearly to remove the speck from your brother's eye" (**Matthew 7:1-5**).

Jesus taught a lot about mirrors, and he implored his listeners to look into them often. One of our biggest problems as humans is that, when it comes to detecting our own flaws and faults, we look through the wrong end of the binoculars. Try it sometime and you'll discover that what should be real clear is barely detectable. But when it comes to picking others apart and seeing their weaknesses, we become scientists. We get our microscopes out, put people on a slide and look long and hard to spot even the slightest sign of sinful behavior. If that's unsuccessful, we'll locate the telescope and bring into focus those far away objects in others that clearly show why we're not at fault. We love our scopes, and unfortunately they work perfectly every time. They offer clear images to help us feel better about ourselves. They reveal the tiniest of impure motives in others that momentarily take us off the hook.

Every last one of us owns at least one of these powerful scopes of justification and rationalization. Jesus tells us to put them away. Or better yet, keep them out but only use them on yourself. Put yourself under the microscope and look for strange little creatures of bitterness, selfishness and envy. Turn the telescope around on yourself and see if you have any rings of anger, hatred and deceit circling your personal planet.

That first sermon had a lot to offer. It touched on issues many had rarely considered. In wrapping up this sermon, Jesus filled his hearers with more clear and colorful illustrations. He used pigs and pearls to preach on caution (**Matthew 7:6**). He heralded the three-step plan of ask, seek and knock to teach people about boldness and persistence in prayer (**Matthew 7:7-8**). He contrasted bread with stone and then fish with snakes to communicate the heart of a good and giving God (**Matthew 7:9-11**). He introduced the Golden Rule, wrapping up the entire Old Testament in just one sentence (**Matthew 7:12**). He revealed two open gates leading to people's final destination and warned them about the width of both (**Matthew 7:13-14**). He told people to look beyond the wooly outside of some so-called sheep and look at the facts like Little Red Riding Hood (**Matthew 7:15-20**). He made it clear that "Lord, Lord" must line up exactly with "life, life" or people would be in for the shock of their lives on judgment day (**Matthew 7:21-23**). He made his last point with a blueprint for building a house of life in anticipation of bad weather (**Matthew 7:24-27**). And when he finished, the crowds who were privileged to be there went home amazed at the words Jesus spoke and the way that he spoke them (**Matthew 7:28-29**).

There were many more sermons in Jesus' three-year stint on the preaching circuit. To those bogged down in the legalism of their current tradition, Jesus spoke about a rest for the soul and a release from the burdens of life (**Matthew 11:28-30**). To those hurling accusations about Jesus keeping company with the devil, he coined a phrase that has been copied for centuries: *"A house divided against itself cannot stand"* (**Matthew 12:25-28**). He taught the impossibility of adults making it to heaven without mimicking a child's humility (**Matthew 18:1-3**). He cooked up a sizzling rebuke for all hypocrites with images of gnats, camels, dead men's bones, whitewashed tombs and snakes, yet seasoned it with a closing reminder about how much he had loved and longed to save each one of them (**Matthew 23:1-39**). He revealed the definition of "good" in the story of the Good Samaritan (**Luke 10:25-37**). He cleared up the burden of guilt in regard to birth defects (**John 9:1-3**), opened our eyes to the truth of spiritual blindness (**John 9:39-41**), warned about the dangers of emotionalism and altar calls (**Luke 14:25-33**), prepared people for persecution (**John 15:18-27**) and excited us with the credentials of the Holy Spirit (**John 16:5-16**). He constantly taught about the reality of God's love while never diminishing the reality of hell (**Mark 9:42-49**). He never deleted a challenging point from one of his sermons when warned a critic or two might be present (**Matthew 23:1-39**). He never pouted or questioned his strategy when all but a few deserted him (**John 6:60-67**), and he never boasted about his church-growth success when thousand decided to stay. He never swerved erratically to avoid an awkward interrogation (**Matthew 18:23-27**), yet he was always aware of a trap by the enemy that deserved a silent reply (**Matthew 22:15-22**). He didn't apologize for who he was and what he expected. He was, to put it simply, all about God and getting God's message out to as many as possible.

Yes, the baby grew up and had something to say. He had a lot to say! And every time he spoke, the crowds were amazed. Even Jesus' enemies knew they had met their match. So they did the only thing they could possibly do to shut him up—they killed him. But two-thousand years later, we still hear Jesus preach in the pages of the Bible. The faithful few who hung on his every word knew his teachings were from God, unparalleled with anything they had ever heard before. And they knew it would never be matched or surpassed. So his disciples made sure that those born in future generations would be able to come to the same conclusions as those who were there to hear him in person: *"No one ever spoke the way this man does."*

Then he got into the boat and his disciples followed him. Without warning, a furious storm came up on the lake, so that the waves swept over the boat. But Jesus was sleeping. The disciples went and woke him, saying, "Lord save us! We're going to drown!" He replied, "You of little faith, why are you so afraid?" Then he got up and rebuked the winds and the waves, and it was completely calm.
The men were amazed and asked, "What kind of man is this? Even the winds and the waves obey him."

–Matthew 8:23-27

CHAPTER SEVENTEEN

What Kind of Man Is This?

It truly was a set-up. With his series of miraculous billboards, God was slowing down the fast and furious freeway traffic called life. Each bright and enormous sign was being used to entice all the hectic and hurried drivers to slow down, move over to the far right lane, take the next exit and check out what seemed too good to be true in the man they called Jesus. And it worked!

The miracles Jesus performed were signaling many of the previously uninterested to at least drive slow enough to catch a glimpse of his amazing activities. And the startling displays of the unexplainable convinced many of them to stop and stay around long enough to hear what he had to say.

Most of the Jews at the time of Jesus were content living in their compromised peace with Rome, for the most part being allowed to continue in their worship of God and the observance of their sacred laws and traditions. They wanted nothing to do with any takeover attempt that might take away their present harmony with Caesar. But many of those sentiments began to change when the weather began changing with no meteorological explanation and corpses began dancing at the funerals Jesus attended.

"So Jesus, you say you have some important matters we need to hear? Okay,

we'll stay and listen to what you have to say. Anybody who can do what you've been doing must have a few tricks up their sleeve that Rome hasn't seen before."

So thousands stayed around to hear Jesus speak. That had been the plan from the beginning. Drop a miracle into their laps and then drop the truth into their hearts. Whether the miracle was in front of a few or in the sight of the masses huddled on a mountainside, the Jesus billboards were always attention-getters. Some said they were clear proof that divine power was present. Some were saying the miracles were reminiscent of those done by the great prophets of old. But they all hoped they were the ultimate sign that God was ready to make a move on behalf of his people.

The miracles of Jesus sparked the interest of a typical Israelite the way rumors of miraculous events arouse our curiosity today (**1 Corinthians 1:22**). You know exactly what I mean when you're in the checkout line at the grocery store and venture a quick glance at the headline in the newspaper you would never buy. Here's one I came across a while ago: **Noah's Ark Found on Mars.**

I must admit that I wanted to buy a copy that day and read up on this incredible discovery. It did get me thinking some wild and crazy thoughts for a brief moment. But you know as well as I do that the ark isn't in outer space. Why the next thing we'll hear is that Noah's two dogs are living on Pluto. That's not really possible, is it?

If someone came to my home, told me about their miracle-cure for baldness, touched my head three times and turned desert into rain forest, I'm pretty sure I'd invite them back to hear what they had to say about more important matters in life. Anybody who can do what Rogaine and regular prayers for hair restoration haven't accomplished the past thirty-five years deserves at least some of my undivided attention.

In like manner, people flocked to Jesus. What did they see that caused them to later listen to his messages more carefully? What was it with these miracles that left so many with undeniable evidence that every word from the mouth of the miracle-maker could be fully trusted? Let's take a look at the miracle on the lake described in the beginning of this chapter and ask ourselves the same question the apostles did after witnessing it: *"What kind of man is this?"*

It had been a typical day for Jesus and his apostles, spending much of the morning and afternoon with the masses and teaching them the word of God. Even Jesus was becoming physically worn down with the rigorous schedule and signaled for a ministry time-out. So off to the boat they went, a favorite getaway from the demanding crowds. The weather had been fine that day, all the way through the late afternoon and into the early evening. No storms were in the forecast or on the horizon, and it appeared to be the perfect opportunity to retreat, refresh and regroup for more Jesus-mania ahead. It wasn't long before Jesus nodded off to sleep in the bottom of the boat, resting comfortably on a soft cushion and grabbing some needed rest before shore and an awaiting throng of admirers and those hoping for a chance to be healed (**Mark 4:38**).

Then it happened. The fishermen in the boat had warned the others of the occasional storm that would batter the lake, but this did nothing to prepare them for the terrifying experience about to take place. It was supposed to be relaxation time for the apostles. They had anticipated a calm evening, dropping anchor somewhere in the middle of the lake and taking in the spectacular sunset that would display its splendor in a few hours. It would be one of the best nights for them in quite some time, and they were especially grateful for their Master's sensitivity to their ever-increasing workload. But their perfect world soon ended with the arrival of the perfect storm. And the perfect one who lay asleep would soon wake up and turn their chaos and fears of imminent death into the best boat trip of their entire lives and a ride they would never forget.

Light rain began to fall but lasted only seconds before large droplets of hail were pummeling the boat and the disciples on board. The gale-force winds made it impossible to steady the boat, so the men simply tried to steady themselves and keep from falling overboard. Massive amounts of water from the approaching waves began to fill the boat, and bucketing and bailing efforts became useless. At this rate, it wouldn't be long before the boat would sink, and if that happened, they would all most likely drown. Swimming to safety wasn't an option as the seas were too rough to overcome for even the best swimmers. Boats able to withstand the elements were nowhere in sight, and certainly no rescue attempt could be expected during the fierce downpour.

What could the disciples do now? No human effort was going to help turn the tide as the wind and rain were increasing in strength. The sky was growing more ominous, brightened only by the frequent and nearby bolts of lightning. Only God could intervene now. Jonah's trip overboard came to mind, but none of the apostles were convinced a big enough fish lived in those waters. Prayers had been frantically sent upward since the storm set in, but the heavens kept answering with more rain. So they woke up Jesus. Just exactly what they expected him to do isn't certain, but they were surely out of other options.

"Lord, save us! We're going to drown" (**Matthew 8:25**).

"Teacher, don't you care if we drown?" (**Mark 4:38**).

Jesus was in the middle of a nap and they were in the middle of the biggest crisis of their lives! Perhaps that's what Jesus was hoping for all along. Was this storm the only way the men could come to appreciate whom they had been hanging out with the past year or so? So Jesus woke up, and with a loud lullaby, rocked the storm to sleep. High-flying kites soaring in similar winds would have suddenly plummeted to the ground. What had felt like a hurricane was now a hush. As quick as the storm had come, it had disappeared even faster. The storm stoppage was so sudden, even the rainbow remained backstage.

With only a few words, Jesus told the wind to get a grip and the rain to take a hike. Then it was time to talk to his disciples.

"Why are you so afraid? Do you still have no faith?" (**Mark 4:40**).

And on their way to shore, the apostles asked themselves and each other the same question—*"What kind of man is this?"*

Here are some other ways the question could have been phrased.

"Has a man ever done this before?"

"Could a man do what we saw being done today?"

"Since when does a man have complete control over nature?"

"Is Jesus just a man?"

"Is Jesus the Son of God?"

"Is this God in our boat?"

They were rapidly moving in that direction with each glance

toward the bright, blue skies they enjoyed while rowing back to shore. Jesus had done it again. Would he ever miss? Every paralyzed man he told to walk, walked perfectly without follow-up therapy. Every demon he told to depart, left immediately while saluting him as the Son of God. Every leper he touched was cured on the spot. And now it's the weather!

But for the twelve apostles, this miracle was different because it was all about them. They were saved. They didn't drown. They were the recipients of a Jesus rescue mission. And they had never been so personally grateful for the power they had witnessed from their leader only moments after waking him up from a nap.

What conclusions would you have made about Jesus if you had been on that boat? How would your life have changed? Would you have decided to finally believe his claims even though they still seemed a bit bizarre? Would you have acted differently during the next storm you encountered? Would you have watched Jesus a bit more closely knowing you were watching God? Would you have ever doubted a future promise made by him? Would you have been prouder to tell your friends and family about him?

This miracle was similar to all the other miracles of Jesus. It would not only produce goose pimples, it would produce proof. It would not only bring about bewilderment, it would bring about belief. It would not only cause people to quiver, it would cause them to question— what kind of man is this? Let's take a closer look at this miracle and do our best to capture the same amazement as the disciples did that day.

First, the storm came without warning. The disciples had no idea it was coming. There were no signs of foul weather, and they welcomed being out on the lake and away from the crowds for at least a little while.

Second, it was a furious squall. Thirteen miles long and eight miles wide, this was no small lake. Surrounded on three sides by mountains and cliffs, the lake is situated in a bowl up to 3,500 feet in depth from the bottom of the lake to the top of the Golan Heights. With the air temperature dropping rapidly in the afternoon, it's not uncommon for an avalanche of cool air to flow rapidly downhill, resulting in violent windstorms on the lake. This storm wasn't planning to just calmly subside unless the one who controlled the weather said it was.

Third, the storm ended abruptly. The rains didn't lighten up, they left altogether. The wind didn't slowly diminish, it ceased completely. The dark skies didn't turn to blue over the next few minutes, they appeared in an instant. The waves didn't go from five feet to three, the water went flat. Something supernatural stopped the storm in a most spectacular way.

Fourth, the storm stopped the moment Jesus said it would. Was that a mere coincidence? Was this just a lucky attempt at weather changing? Or was the voice of Jesus the same voice the rain had been accustomed to hearing for centuries? Did the wind obey his voice of authority just like it had been doing since the beginning? Was the invisible one who controlled the world's weather also riding with them in the boat?

All of these questions gave the apostles their answer—God is with us! This and every other miracle Jesus performed left convincing proof of his deity and little room for other possibilities. In these miracles, Jesus would make it next to impossible for them (and us as well) to cling to humanistic explanations.

The water-to-wine miracle was being confirmed by everyone at the wedding reception (**John 2:1-11**). An invalid of 38 years was cured by the touch of Jesus, and those who knew him knew it was real (**John 5:1-15**). A man blind from birth was given sight by Jesus, and medical explanations couldn't be brought to light (**John 9:1-33**). Lazarus was dead for four days before coming back to life, and no medical examiner was going to come forward and say he had only been in a deep coma (**John 11:38-44**).

My personal favorite is a miracle we never actually see occur in the Scriptures but can be confident it took place. During a discussion on taxes and the need for Jesus to pay his, Peter was given direction on how to locate the funds to cover the bill for both of them.

"But so that we may not offend them, go to the lake and throw out your line. Take the first fish you catch; open its mouth and you will find a four-drachma coin. Take it and give it to them for my tax and yours" (**Matthew 17:24-27**).

If you believe this miracle actually took place, as I do, what can you say but "Wow"! How did Jesus know that one fish, out of perhaps hundreds of thousands of fish in the lake at that time, would have swallowed a four-drachma coin? And even if he knew which fish it was, how would he know Peter was going to drop his line in the water at just the right time, in just the right place and catch just the right fish? Maybe Jesus caused the coin to land in the mouth of that fish at the exact moment Peter snagged it. Maybe Jesus summoned the fish by name and led it beneath Peter's line to surrender its life and what was in its mouth. Did Jesus create the coin from nothing the moment he knew Peter would land his first catch of the day? How did Peter know where to go and when to drop his line? How did Jesus know where Peter would go and when he would drop his line? But none of these questions really matter if you calculate the sum of all the miracles of Jesus—he could do whatever he wanted, whenever he wanted, wherever he wanted, however he wanted and for whomever he wanted.

The miracles of Jesus were never attempted in the hope they could somehow be accomplished. Jesus never gave it the good old college try, and he was never told "better luck next time." His miracles were perfect and provable all the time! Most of the rain didn't stop falling, but all of it. Most of the wind didn't stop blowing, but all of it. Most of the waves weren't tamed, but all of them. Most of the disease didn't disappear, but all of it. Most of the dead person didn't come back to life, but all of him.

If you also consider the motives behind the miracles, Jesus is even more amazing. It was always about bringing hope and healing to those he touched. And his last recorded miracle was even performed on behalf of an enemy, as he restored the severed ear of a soldier who had come to arrest him (**Luke 22:49-51**). Even his critics spoke about his unbelievable displays of power, but sadly gave credit most of the time to the devil and the dark side.

God never forces people to believe in him. And he'll never make anybody believe in Jesus just so they'll follow him. But he will give every individual plenty of really good reasons to do both. And the miracles of Jesus are at or near the top of that list!

When Jesus saw her weeping, and the Jews who had come along with her also weeping, he was deeply moved in spirit and troubled. "Where have you laid him?" he asked. "Come and see, Lord," they replied. Jesus wept. Then the Jews said, "See how he loved him."

—John 11:33-36

CHAPTER EIGHTEEN

Jesus Wept

It had been a long four days for the two sisters. They were overwhelmed by the constant reminders of the sad reality neither of them wanted to face. Relatives and friends had come from nearby towns to pay last respects to their deceased brother, Lazarus, a highly regarded man in the village of Bethany. Some had brought food for the family. Others shared tears or listened compassionately to the grieving sisters as they shared their pain. Many relayed memories of special interactions they had engaged in with Lazarus, ones that would hopefully bring a rare smile to Mary and Martha.

Jesus still hadn't arrived, and Mary and Martha were deeply troubled by his unexplained delay. They had sent for him earlier when the first signs of failing health appeared in their brother. Certainly, they thought, if Jesus could get there quickly he could fix whatever the doctors said was too late to fix. They had seen him do it many times in the past with complete strangers, but Lazarus was a dear friend. Surely that love and their faith in his ability to remove the dreaded disease would lead to a cure. But Jesus didn't come. Had Mary and Martha done something to irritate him? Had Lazarus angered him recently by something he had done? Had they completely misread the man they believed to be the greatest example of love they had ever encountered?

Those four days seemed like four months to Mary and Martha. The visitors certainly meant well, but it was all so very draining. Even people they didn't know that well were stopping by, saying "I'm so sorry" and "If there's anything we can do, please let us know." It was kind, but it just wasn't enough. They wanted their brother back. He was their strength and had been for many years. How would they manage without his love and care? And if they couldn't have Lazarus back, at the very least they really needed to see Jesus. Maybe he could help them come to terms with the death of their beloved brother. Jesus had been there during earlier times of crisis in their lives, and he had brought peace on every occasion. But now, in their most difficult hour, he was nowhere to be found. Even a few of the guests were contributing to the sisters' growing doubts and dismay about Jesus' absence.

Mary and Martha were trying to hang on to the memories of love they had experienced with Jesus since he had entered their lives. But questioning comments along with their personal angst were being used by Satan to loosen their grip. Each time they remembered the sight of their brother's lifeless body, they felt deeply hurt and disappointed by Jesus' unexpected delay. No longer was saving their brother's life a possibility. They just wanted an explanation. So they waited. And they waited some more. Then word finally came. Jesus was on his way to Bethany. Martha wasted no time and hurried off to meet him before he arrived (**John 11:20**).

"Lord, if you had been here . . ." (**John 11:21**).

Martha's cautious attempt to place blame for her bother's death on his tardiness didn't bother Jesus. Without flinching, he spoke of Lazarus rising again and then dealt with Martha's misunderstanding of that resurrection promise and plan for her brother.

Martha wasted no time and hurried back home to let Mary know that Jesus was coming and wanted to see her. After hearing Martha's report, Mary rushed off to find Jesus. She was desperate to open her heart to him and reveal her most anxious thoughts to the one she called Lord. In days past, her desire to open her heart and listen to his teachings had been appreciated by Jesus (**Luke 10:38-42**). But now, she was feeling the need to speak her mind.

"Lord, if you had been here . . ." (**John 11:32**).

Mary was weeping as she spoke. Many others who followed Mary were weeping as well. Martha had spent more time crying than not the past four days. Profound sadness hovered over the town as one of Bethany's brightest and best had been taken from them. Many of its residents were shocked and grief-stricken and couldn't imagine life without Lazarus. They had also wondered about the delay of the one who had the power to prevent this awful outcome.

"Could not he who opened the eyes of the blind man have kept this man from dying?" (**John 11:37**).

The answer was a resounding "yes" in most of their minds. But the bigger question was "why." Why didn't Jesus come when he could have done something about the illness?

Jesus was well aware of the quiet criticism. And he could see the tears and feel the pain of those affected by the tragedy. So Jesus did what God had been doing in regard to his creation for thousands of years when they just didn't get it—he wept (**John 11:35**).

He could have rebuked them for their unjustified bitterness. He could have simply performed the resurrection miracle from a distance and been on his merry way. He could have walked away and done nothing, justified by his knowledge of Lazarus' positive eternal condition. He could have told them to toughen up and learn an important lesson—that pain and suffering from the death of a loved-one are all part of the necessary challenges of earthly life and a call for those left behind to focus all the more on heaven. Or he could have taught a long lesson on trusting God in trying times.

But Jesus did here what was consistent with what he had done since the beginning of his ministry—he loved. Jesus knew all along what he was about to do. But for Jesus, it had never been just about doing. It was always a whole lot more about loving. He always lowered himself to other people's levels and listened to their pains and fears. After all, that was the plan all along—God reached down, came down and sat down to see if he could offer a helping hand.

I think one of the reasons Jesus wept that day was because he knew the people there were grieving. And that was a very familiar feeling for him as well (**Genesis 6:5-7**). He knew it had been a rough four days for all the people there, and he wanted them to know that he understood what they had been forced to endure, even though he wasn't physically present. God has always cared about our pain, and Jesus came to make that truth known in flesh and blood, this time with tears.

It was love that brought Jesus to Bethany that afternoon, and it was love that led him to the tomb to wake up Lazarus. It had to be something extraordinary for Jesus to call Lazarus away from the Paradise party he'd been enjoying those past four days. Jesus had already changed his earthly life and eternal destiny, but for some reason, he felt the need to bring him back to a world full of trouble and an appointment for another dying day. What could explain this strange decision? What was moving in the heart of Jesus and troubling him so? We'll never know for sure, but since love was the driving force in all that Jesus did, here are some options.

Did Jesus have concerns about Mary's future faithfulness to him if Lazarus were to be left alone? Did Jesus see a bitter root of doubt and resentment growing inside of Mary? Would Satan gladly use it to tempt her to turn away from Jesus altogether? Was raising Lazarus the only way to raise Mary's spirits and keep her from returning to the old life that had brought her so much emptiness and pain?

Maybe Jesus did it all for Martha. He knew about Martha's tendency to worry and fret. Perhaps Jesus could see a nervous breakdown on her horizon without Lazarus in her life to help stabilize her anxious ways.

Could the miracle have been performed for the townspeople of Bethany? Maybe those in Bethany weren't quite spiritual enough to accept this date of death for Lazarus, and bitterness and blaming God would have ended their quest of pursuing Jesus. Did Jesus raise Lazarus just to give them more time to grow in their faith so they'd be ready to accept the next difficult-to-understand death in their town?

Perhaps there was someone among the mourners who would have wandered away from being a disciple of Jesus if not for the resurrection miracle. Did Jesus do it all for that single sheep?

Maybe Lazarus had a reclusive neighbor whom he had nearly convinced to become a disciple of Jesus. Maybe that neighbor needed one more lesson before answering the call, and Lazarus was the only one he had ever trusted enough to come into his home and get into his heart.

Perhaps Jesus raised Lazarus because he wanted to give his critics one more chance to change their stance before voicing support to eliminate him. Not that Jesus was looking to save himself from the cross. In Jesus' mind, that was a foregone conclusion. Instead, he would do it to grant those who wanted him dead a golden opportunity to avoid making a decision that would harden their hearts for good.

Love was the reason Jesus did everything. Who else would touch a leper when they could have cured him from afar? It was love that put Jesus' hand on rotting flesh to give that leper the one thing he needed more than smooth skin (**Mark 1:40-42**).

Love was the reason he told ten-thousand angels on rescue watch not to worry or bother breaking in to save him from his painful future (**Matthew 26:51-54**).

It was love that led Jesus to notice a widow drop two cents into a billion-dollar bucket and make her feel like a million bucks (**Luke 21:1-4**)?

It was love that led Jesus to discuss the marital status of the woman at the well (**John 4:16-18**), and it was love that totally bypassed the social order of his day to give her a chance to change.

It was love that kept an adulterous woman alive while Jesus killed the pride of her firing squad (**John 8:2-11**).

It was love that steered the hands of Jesus to wash the dirty feet of his followers (**John 13:1-17**).

It was love that moved Jesus to say "Father forgive them" to those mocking him at his crucifixion (**Luke 23:32-34**).

Regardless of someone's status in life, their reputation with others or their relationship with him, when people were in the presence of Jesus, they could count on being loved. Whether they were wealthy or woefully poor; a fellow Jew or a foreigner; distinguished or demon-possessed; pure or a prostitute; very religious or very rarely thinking about God; a dear friend or a determined foe; a member of the family or a member of the mob who called out for his death; a baby in his arms or a bystander in his face—all were loved by Jesus.

If you happen to be familiar with the words of Paul in his first letter to the church in Corinth (**1 Corinthians 13:4-8**), you wouldn't be surprised if instead it read like this:

Jesus was always patient, Jesus was always kind. Jesus never envied, never boasted and was never proud. He was never rude, he was never self-seeking, he was never easily angered and he never kept a record of wrongs. Jesus never delighted in evil but always rejoiced with the truth. Jesus always protected, always trusted, always hoped and always persevered. Jesus never failed.

In running terms, his teachings got Jesus out of the starting blocks. His miracles put him in full stride. But it was love that broke the tape. And when Jesus looked back, nobody else was even in the race.

For surely it is not angels he helps, but Abraham's descendants. For this reason, he had to be made like his brothers in every way, in order that he might become a merciful and faithful high priest, in service to God, and that he might make atonement for the sins of the people. Because he himself suffered when he was tempted, he is able to help those who are being tempted.

—Hebrews 2:16-18

CHAPTER NINETEEN

God Was One of Us

I don't think you really understand what I'm feeling."
"I really need to talk with someone who can relate."
"You just don't get me, do you?"

Most of us have probably shared similar statements of frustration at one time or another. Sometimes, those words were absolutely true. At other times, self-pity or sadness brought them out of our hearts and into the public arena. Yet regardless of what our motives were in sharing those feelings, it is definitely true that all of us tend to do better emotionally and spiritually when we feel connected with and understood by another human being.

Just look at the evidence in your life. Don't you have more desire to spend time with people who can relate to you on a number of levels? For many of us, if we have even one thing in common with somebody, that one thing is often enough to motivate us to pursue some type of relationship with them. If we have more than one thing in common, we're likely to invest time and energy into that relationship. If we relate on a number of levels or have many similarities, we often become close friends. And in some cases, these commonalities lead to a lifetime commitment of marriage.

True, some of these similarities could be considered shallow or unspiritual in nature. Nevertheless, most of us will at least attempt to build a friendship based upon these interests. Things such as where we're from, where we've lived, where we went to school, what we studied in school, what jobs we've had, whether we enjoy the same sports or have the same hobbies, whether we listen to the same type of music or like the same kind of movies—these are often launching pads for developing relationships.

Now granted, there are more important areas of similarity we will discover in others that can help us grow closer to them—things such as experiencing the same physical challenge growing up, enduring a similar tragedy or losing a close friend or member of the family.

For example, if you suffered through a difficult childhood because of any form of abuse or neglect, or if your parents got divorced and it ripped your heart in two, who better to understand your current crisis than someone who's felt those same feelings of despair.

If you've been divorced, aren't you more interested in sharing your life story with someone who knows all about the emptiness that follows when the divorce becomes final? To begin rebuilding your life, wouldn't you rather seek help and comfort from someone who knows how very scary it is to do something like go on a first date after officially becoming single again?

If you're having difficulty conceiving a child, isn't it more comforting to spend time with a friend who can totally understand the lump in your throat and the tear in your eye whenever a pregnancy announcement is read at church? Wouldn't her heart quickly engage with yours if you shared how you felt when you noticed a pregnant woman walking through the grocery store?

If your financial picture gets completely out of focus, what type of individual will you look for to discuss recovery plans? Would it be the financial planner who was one step from bankruptcy earlier in their life but has since bounced back? Or would you prefer the child of a millionaire who studied economics in college but has never felt the need to balance their checkbook?

If you were entertaining thoughts of giving up your walk with God and following the ways of the world appeared to be the easier option, wouldn't you try to locate the person who left the Lord once but is now back on track? Wouldn't you want to set up an appointment with them and hear their story? It's not that the person who's never considered a "return to Egypt" couldn't help some, but can they relate to you like the other individual? Wouldn't the prodigal son or daughter be better equipped to bring you some much-needed perspective on how incredibly easy but unbelievably foolish it is to buy into the lie about how awesome it is on the outside?

Now I'm not saying it would be right to listen to anyone who will minimize the need for you to deal with your challenges in a godly manner. Nor would I encourage you to search for someone who won't deal with the sin in your life, the sin that could very well be a major part of your problem. But sometimes we just need someone who's "been there, done that" to help us be who we need to be and do what we need to do. God knew this was how most of us think and operate, so he became one of us.

Unfortunately, most of us don't think of God in this way. We often think the exact opposite and believe God can't relate at all because he's never walked in our shoes. Oh, but he has. He knows all about our shoes. His shoes also walked through pain and suffering. His shoes had to dance around temptation just like ours do. And his shoes were sometimes tight and very uncomfortable.

God knows how tough life can be. He's not unsympathetic about the challenges we face. He's not quick to call us quitters or wimps when we decide for a brief moment to side with Satan and slip on shoes from his store. He knows how tough the devil and the dark side can be. He knows all about the seductive sales pitches coming from Satan's shoe store. He was tempted to purchase a pair on occasion, but instead kept the perfect ones he had from the beginning.

Nothing has happened in your life that Jesus can't relate to on some level. Anything you are currently experiencing, Jesus has been there in a similar way. Sure, he may not have had the exact experience, but he can relate to the emotion or the temptation that accompanies the situation.

No, he didn't deal with old age, but he always knew that death was near. No, he was never confined to a wheelchair, but he was definitely bound to the flesh. No, he wasn't married, but he can totally relate to the pain of marital crisis or divorce because he often dealt with the emotions stemming from people wanting to quit on him. And he definitely knows the devastating feeling of a once-special relationship coming to an abrupt end. No, he never experienced the extreme disappointment of finding out about a miscarriage or a stillbirth, but he does know the sadness of seeing someone he loved come so close to becoming a member of his spiritual family, only to watch that individual change their mind just short of the new birth.

So please don't minimize this piece of incredible news—God was one of us! God really does know the feeling of being a stranger on a bus. And what could be more challenging than Jesus having to be one-hundred percent human while hanging on to the fullness of his deity, all while the devil and the dark forces of evil were doing everything in their power to derail the plan.

In his daily struggle to push away pride, how many times was Jesus tempted to pat himself on the back for another perfect day? How often did he want to consider himself better than others when he knew all along that nobody else was even close (**Philippians 2:3-11**)? How many times did it become necessary for Jesus to dig deep and fight hard to erase any notion of clinging proudly to being equal with God? When did making himself nothing get eerily close to the point of getting really old? Just how hard was it for Jesus to turn away from desiring and reveling in the compliments that came his way?

Had it ever been so easy to allow anger and self-righteousness to well up in his heart as when he saw the impulsive nature of man? With huge crowds chanting for him to declare his candidacy for King of Israel, Jesus must have entertained thoughts of taking the road most traveled, especially as he contemplated how the crowds would dramatically change their tune a few years later and demand his crucifixion.

So God really does get it! He was one of us. The mere fact that Jesus left heaven and landed on foreign soil means he can relate to every one of us in some way. But let's close the chapter by considering some other challenges Jesus faced in his life on Earth. Let's see if it's possible that Jesus might just know exactly what we're feeling whenever we face our own struggles and challenges.

He had no beauty or majesty to attract us to him, nothing in his appearance that we should desire him (**Isaiah 53:2**).

Average Looks

Having to constantly view the beauty of models and movie stars can cause most of us to wish we had been swimming in a different gene pool. Yes, the truth remains that the vast majority of us are a whole lot closer to average and so-so than we are to awesome and stunning. Not many take second glances our way. It's either our forehead is too shiny, our nose is too big, our ears stick out, our chin is too pointed, our hair is too thin, our teeth are too crooked, our cheeks are too rosy or our wrinkles are too obvious. If I missed your facial flaw, write it down in the margin. When you're finished with that, come join the rest of us ordinary people. But not to worry—Jesus will be there, too.

What was it with his looks that prompted the Spirit to indicate to the prophet Isaiah that there was nothing in his appearance that we should desire him? Sorry to disappoint you, but God didn't tell us. Forget the picture of Jesus in the hallway of your home that you saw growing up, the one with the near-perfect facial features and the long, flowing hair, and focus instead on average. That's as much as God has chosen to tell us about the physical appearance of Jesus. But don't be too concerned that you'll never know exactly what Jesus looked like. Doesn't just knowing he was average looking make it a little easier to take your insecurities to him?

Could knowing that Jesus understands the hurt that comes from being overlooked because of looks help you move beyond the recent promotion you should have received at your workplace that was given instead to the more attractive, less-qualified candidate? Could understanding that Jesus had to learn contentment with the mirror's revelation every time he readied himself for the day help you to stop fretting about what you can't really change this side of a plastic surgeon? Maybe a brother or two was blessed with better looks than Jesus. Maybe all four were finer in appearance. Could this help you to once and for all eliminate your envy of a sibling's luck with their looks? Could the fact that God in the flesh chose to be average in appearance help you realize that looks aren't everything, and in truth, looks are really nothing? Be encouraged by the truth that Jesus fully understands the emotional challenge of being just another face in the crowd.

The Jews answered him, "Aren't we right in saying that you are a Samaritan and demon-possessed" (**John 8:48**)?

Unfair Treatment

It would be naive to think that this was the first time Jesus got hit with this verbal jab. More than likely, this slanderous slug to the gut landed often, beginning in his growing-up years. Because of Mary's unusual pregnancy, it seemed to be a simple conclusion to most people that Joseph was not the father of Jesus. Instead, people were quite sure Mary had succumbed to the lustful advances of a Gentile man and that her fiancé, Joseph, felt sorry for her, forgave her and took her to be his wife. When she finally gave birth to Jesus, Joseph humbly decided to occupy the role of the child's father. Soon, the unenviable label of Samaritan (half Jewish, half Gentile) was placed upon Jesus. It certainly couldn't have been a comfortable label to wear for Jesus since most of his time was spent around full-blooded Jews who despised what they considered to be the lesser Samaritans. It was this belief about Jesus, combined with what many were calling a hilarious cover-up in calling himself the Son of God, that made Jesus a prime target for trash talk.

If you've ever been handed a name that you never asked for or deserved, Jesus knows your pain. Whether the unwanted label was given to you as a statement about some physical deficiency, a slam on your family's reputation or the result of a one-time lapse in good judgment, name-calling never does much for our self-esteem as children, and it often follows us right on into adulthood. Just don't forget that Jesus is following you, too. He gets it. He hurts for you and with you, and he wants to help you get past any roadblock you're now facing on your journey back to self-worth.

The unfair treatment continued throughout Jesus' life. He was accused of gluttony, drunkenness, carousing with loose women, intentionally deceiving people for personal gain, representing Satan himself, not upholding the Jewish law, rebelling against Rome, not paying his taxes, being insane and probably a lot of other things that aren't recorded in the Scriptures. The epitome of the wrongful attacks on Jesus came as religious leaders wove together a series of half-truths and lies about him, presented that false evidence in a completely illegal trial, condemned him to death and convinced the Romans powers to crucify him as though he were a hardened criminal. Even while Jesus hung in pain on the cross, false accusations and slanderous statements were being hurled at him by those who passed by his execution site.

Unfair treatment was a part of Jesus' life from the moment he was conceived to the moment he uttered *'It is finished'* (**Luke 23:46**). Even to this day, people continue to treat him unfairly. Many make false statements about him with little or no knowledge of his actual life. Some claim his entire persona is a complete fabrication. And others regularly shout out his name in their outbursts of anger or moments of rage.

Then Jesus entered a house, and again a crowd gathered, so that he and his disciples were not even able to eat. When his family heard about this, they went to take charge of him, for they said, "He is out of his mind" (**Mark 3:20-21**).

Family Challenges

Even his own kinfolk had trouble understanding Jesus at times. They actually had concluded on one occasion that Jesus had lost his mind and needed to be rescued from the peril that awaited him. It was a first-century form of family intervention as they went to relieve him of his Messianic duties.

Perhaps you can relate to Jesus. Maybe you've felt forced to walk through life carrying an umbrella in anticipation of your parents or people closest to you raining on your next planned parade. Maybe this is how you felt when you knew you were headed in the right direction but your parents were totally convinced you had taken a wrong turn somewhere. It's that feeling you get when the very people you most want in your corner are the same ones who have suddenly resigned from being your trainer.

Maybe you're there today and your parents think you've lost your mind and lost your right to keep the family name.

Maybe your commitment to Jesus has been deemed too radical and it produces friction when you can't be with your family for the length of time they've deemed appropriate.

Maybe the man of your dreams wasn't the man of theirs and now dreams of family unity are gone.

Maybe your parents wanted you to attend their alma mater and your choice of a different college was deemed foolish.

Maybe your parents are disappointed with the career choice you made. Maybe they pushed for doctor or lawyer but you pursued teacher or social worker. Now you face those "I told you so" looks and comments when you don't have the needed funds for a down payment on the home you'd like to purchase.

Whatever pain you felt, or whatever pain you still carry due to the disappointment of your family, Jesus can relate to your struggles. And best of all, he can help you work through them.

The king was distressed, but because of his oaths and his dinner guests, he ordered that her request be granted and had John the Baptist beheaded in prison (**Matthew 14:9-10**).

When Jesus heard what had happened, he withdrew by boat to a solitary place (**Matthew 14:13**).

Death of a Loved One

For Jesus, this must have been the worst of news. John the Baptist was dead. But John wasn't just a fellow prophet. He was a relative and probably a great friend for many years. Nobody else had the ability to understand all the challenges Jesus faced, but at least John could relate to some. How many times do you suppose they sat down to discuss life and the loneliness of being God's voice to the people? Or the misunderstanding of family and friends who viewed their radical lifestyles as misguided? Who else could Jesus turn to for a listening ear? Who else could he spend time with and be brought closer to God? And now, John was no longer there to be a support to Jesus. And though it can't be proved, many scholars believe that Jesus also suffered the loss of his earthly father, Joseph. If so, that would have been another incredibly difficult time emotionally for Jesus, regardless of what age he was when it happened.

Who was it for you? Who died and left you hurting like never before? When did the gaping hole first appear in your heart? When did you first suffer the pain of an earthly separation? When did you first realize how many tears could be produced in one day? When did you first feel the need to just get away from everything and everybody and a big part of you never wanted to come back?

Perhaps it was a parent or a sibling who died. Maybe it was a grandparent or a really good friend. Maybe it was a child or a close relative. Whoever it was who is no longer with you, and whatever pain you felt when they passed away, or whatever pain you still feel from that separation, Jesus feels it all and understands how it has shaped your life.

He could not do any miracles there, except to lay his hands on a few people and heal them. And he was amazed at their lack of faith (**Mark 6:5-6**).

Disappointment

I'm guessing you've experienced the discouragement of working hard for something but seeing little or nothing placed in the results column. Perhaps you poured out your heart to someone and tried to help them in their pursuit of God, but their heart stayed hard. You spent countless hours in that endeavor, and now you're tempted to feel like it was all a big waste of time. Or perhaps you're tempted to feel that it must have been something you did or didn't do that caused them to turn down the greatest of all invitations. Now you're feeling less and less excited about helping anybody else learn those important truths.

Jesus knows exactly how you feel. He was amazed that people could be so stubborn. He was dumbfounded that people could be ignorant and blind so as not to see who he really was. He couldn't believe his hometown cronies could dismiss his Lord and Savior claims so quickly. Maybe Jesus also had those moments when he started questioning his need to proceed.

So the next time your church invitation is turned down, or when that person you're trying to help decides they can spend their spare time doing something else besides learning about God, or when nothing on your prayer list gets moved to the answered column, bring it before the throne of God because Jesus knows exactly what you're feeling.

So what else can you count on Jesus understanding? Here are some possible answers to that question.

He experienced physical exhaustion (**John 4:6**), needed a nap and took it on a comfortable cushion (**Mark 4:38**). He collapsed in complete despair as he was forced to carry his cross to the crucifixion site (**Matthew 27:32, John 19:17**).

He had intense moments of sadness (**John 11:35**) and emotional despair (**Luke 22:39-44**). He was angry and became upset at people's stubbornness and hardness of heart (**Mark 3:1-5**).

He knows all about being unappreciated. His kindness and ability to cure gave ten lepers a new lease on life, but nine left without saying thanks (**Luke 17:11-19**).

He knows what it's like not to be able to find the time to get away from it all. He understands the challenge of trying to schedule a few moments of fellowship with your two best friends called peace and quiet, and he knows the real frustration of being interrupted when you weren't through visiting (**Mark 6:30-34**).

He experienced the pressure of having to stay calm in a crowd and righteous in a riot (**Mark 2:1-2, 4:1, 14:43-50**). Surely he can help us find peace while trying to find a parking space. Without a doubt, he can understand our anxiety in an unexpected traffic delay.

He knows your desire for wanting to take the easier path and how simple it would be to justify it (**Matthew 26:52-54**).

Jesus knows the lowest levels of loneliness and what it feels like watching friends you should be able to count on not being there for you during your greatest hour of need (**Matthew 26:40-46**).

He knows what it's like having others around you who are trying to set you up to fail (**Matthew 22:15-22**).

He understands what it's like going from most popular to most pathetic in the popularity polls (**Luke 4:22-30, John 6:60-66**).

He felt frustration with the established system of government in his day, and he was unfairly tried and convicted as a result of their decisions (**Matthew 23:1-7, 26:57-58**).

He endured severe emotional anguish and longed for God to provide the easier way out (**Luke 22:39-44**).

And he suffered through intense physical pain for extended periods of time (**Matthew 26:67, 27:26-31**).

You could say Jesus felt it all. Truly, God was one of us.

*For we do not have a high priest who is
unable to empathize with our weaknesses,
but we have one who has
been tempted in every way,
just as we are—yet he did not sin.*

–Hebrews 4:15

CHAPTER TWENTY

Not Even Once

Go ahead and give it your best shot. Make it your all-consuming passion for the next twenty-four hours. Let nothing enter your mind but this one thought: *"I will not sin for the entire day!"* How will you plan on accomplishing that lofty goal? Perhaps you should secretly slip away from the numerous pressures of life and head up into the mountains for the entire day.

Or you could find yourself a reliable partner who has made the same commitment of avoiding sin and you can keep each other as focused as possible throughout the day.

Or you could stay locked in your house all day long, ask other members of your household to do just the opposite, and keep yourself from every possible temptation you typically face in a normal day outside the comforts of your home.

Maybe you could put on a thick blindfold and forbid your eyes from moving your heart away from the narrow road of absolute purity (**1 Thessalonians 4:3-5**).

Maybe you could tightly tape your mouth shut and eliminate your lips from letting loose just once to keep the commandment of speaking *only what is for the building up of others* (**Ephesians 4:29**).

Or why not volunteer to work twenty-four straight hours at the local homeless shelter and serve the needy. Surely you wouldn't think of sinning during your time there because you'll be overwhelmed with gratitude for your blessed life.

Better yet, you could persuade your entire church family to take the challenge and have a twenty-four-hour worship service full of prayer, singing and Scripture reading.

Could you do it? Could you keep your eyes focused, your mouth muzzled, your mind clear and your heart pure for even one day? Honestly, your best bet in reaching this gargantuan goal would be to just go to sleep and not bother waking up for the next twenty-four hours. Go ahead and catch up on all the hours of rest you've been robbed of recently, then wake up and pat yourself on the back for your amazing accomplishment of a day without sin. Then try creating the same scenario the following day and see how long you go before Satan has suckered you into seeking out some silly, short-term pleasure called sin.

Now imagine not sinning for your entire life. For thirty-three years, Jesus turned down the devil's advances and brought honor to God. Not even once did he slip. In my opinion, this is the most incredible accomplishment ever known to man. Nobody else has ever done what Jesus did in delivering a knockout blow to each and every sinful opponent he faced. Nobody else has ever come anywhere close to reaching the highmark of righteousness that Jesus set for how a human should live out their existence. Any attempt to compare any other individual to him is deplorable. Any comment of "you remind me of Jesus" should be shunned, leaving us too embarrassed to respond. Any mention of Mohammad or Buddha in the same category as Jesus is as farfetched as the Earth being flat or war being fun. And any plan to speak of Confucius and Christ in the same breath or on the same level should be permanently shelved.

But what is even more amazing to me about Jesus is the context in which he remained sinless. Jesus wasn't living in total isolation. He didn't hang out for months on end at the Messiah Monastery. He didn't just sneak out for a quick trip to the nearby deli once a week and cross paths with a few wonderful people along the way. He didn't sail his boat on the Sea of Galilee all-day-every-day then put up a "Do Not

Disturb" sign when he docked for the night. People didn't come to Jesus by appointment only. Usually people forced their way into his time and space. He spent just as much time dealing with his enemies as he did teaching his friends. He never wore a bag over his head to maintain purity, and he never avoided conversations or spending time with women to maintain his lust-free status. People rarely understood Jesus, regularly questioned his motives and were looking for ways to make his life as miserable as possible.

Satan had a target on Jesus since his birth in Bethlehem. Who knows how many vicious attacks were launched to destroy Jesus. In the desert, a starving Jesus was the target of the devil's flaming arrows with his seemingly innocent offers of making bread, governing the world and taking leaps from tall buildings to prove God was with him. Three years later in the Garden of Gethsemane, Satan unloaded his entire arsenal upon Jesus while he was in the midst of his deepest sorrow and anticipating the suffering he was about to endure to become the offering acceptable to God for the sins of the world.

Throughout the lifetime of Jesus, Satan had one thought: JUST ONCE! He cleverly had demons positioned at every turn of Jesus. He made personal appearances where the best opportunities were available and often launched hell's fury in the path of Jesus. And all he needed to do was succeed once. One sin would be enough. One sin would end the eternal plan. One sin would increase hell's population by the billions. One sin would send the heavens and the Earth into an eternal frenzy. One sin would cancel all Christmas celebrations. One sin would eliminate all printing orders for Bibles and church hymnals. One sin would end the need for this book. One sin would bring Jesus down to the level of every other man and woman who has ever lived.

But one sin never happened. Not once in private, not once in a crowd. Not once during a heated debate with the Pharisees, not once when thinking quietly to himself. Not once during forty lonely days in the desert with no food and water, not once when enjoying plentiful food and fellowship. Not once when falsely accused, not once when properly identified. Not once when given the cold shoulder, not once when being praised. Not once when looking at a woman, not once when thinking about a woman. Not once when the world's riches were at his disposal, not once when the world's wrath was on his doorstep. Not once when he agonized in physical pain, not once when he enjoyed physical prowess. Not once when his best friends abandoned him, not once when his best friends worshipped him. Not once early in the morning, not once late at night. Not once when nobody was looking, not once when everybody was staring. Not once while lying in bed, not once while walking the busy streets of Jerusalem. Not once when he rebuked, not once when he encouraged. Not once when he was full of energy, not once when he was exhausted. Not once when he was emotionally drained, not once when he was on an emotional high. Not even once!

Add to all of this the fact that Jesus lived with the pressure of knowing he had to remain sinless, even though temptation would visit him constantly, and that you and I, two-thousand years later, were depending upon him to succeed.

Steering clear of sin is no easy task. Even when we set out to do good works, our hearts are constantly being tested and found to be falling short of perfection.

One of those moments for me was when I lived in St. Louis and was helping guide professional baseball fans into various parking areas close to the stadium. It was one of the ways we encouraged church members to raise funds to help them meet their financial pledges for a yearly mission's contribution. Many of the people who helped in this effort had already exceeded their pledges, but they would take the additional amount they were earning and apply it toward someone else in the congregation who was falling short of their personal goal. I had already reached my goal, but I still participated a total of five times. But as I did, I discovered a few troubling things about my heart and quickly realized just how far I still needed to go to be more like Jesus.

On one occasion, I had no real desire to be there. I found myself becoming critical toward some of the church members who were short of their giving goal but still hadn't participated. I saw self-righteousness rise to new heights right before my very eyes. I proudly thought I was better and more spiritual than those individuals, all because I was going above and beyond the expectations I had set for myself in this opportunity to honor God. Sin!

I repented of that bad attitude and looked forward to my next opportunity to help in the fund-raising. This time, I cautiously guarded my heart and refused to consider who was and wasn't there, or how many times they had worked compared to me. Unfortunately, I dropped my shield just long enough to allow Satan the necessary time to carefully aim his bow and shoot his fiery arrows my way, piercing my heart with more pride and arrogance. During the four hours I was helping out, the thought of "I'm sure glad I don't do this for a living" penetrated the spiritual layers of my hearts, seeping into those same invisible chambers that I'd been working to strengthen for years. I began to look down on those who worked full-time as parking attendants, considering myself to be better than them. Sin!

Thank God I fought off those horrendous thoughts. I returned from my sinful journey to once again realize that preacher of the word and parker of the car had equal worth in the eyes of God.

My third opportunity to serve in this capacity started off great. I was determined to stay righteous in the areas I had sinned in earlier, and I felt little or no temptation to return to those ugly thoughts for personal gratification. And just when I was beginning to think the parking lot demons had been cast out and conquered, along came Satan.

On this particular evening, I was helping out in the lot closest to the stadium where many of the wealthiest patrons were parking, along with family members of the players and coaches. Top of the line SUV's, BMW's and Mercedes proceeded my way, and my job was to check each driver's credentials and usher them into the proper area. And then it hit me—the thought I had never thought previously.

"I wonder if these people think I work here full-time or if they know I'm a volunteer?"

"I hope people know I'm doing this to help out the less fortunate."

Can you believe it? Here were complete strangers that I would likely never see again, and I was worried about their impressions of me. What did it matter? Why was that such a big deal to me? Was I again thinking this job was below me? Why should I even care about what people think? If I were really living as a disciple of Jesus, wouldn't I want to let the wealthy folks know that people parking cars were just as important to God as those performing surgeries, and just as special to him as those performing wonders on the field inside the stadium? But wait a minute.

Why did I need to let the wealthy people know anything? Why couldn't I just do my job, smile and be kind to everybody who entered the lot regardless of their income. Why couldn't I just waltz through my four hours of parking lot labor with joy and gratitude, thanking God for the ability to stand for that length of time and for the privilege and honor of helping his kingdom in some small way? Sin!

Believe it or not, I actually looked forward to each of those parking endeavors. I had two more opportunities, and I came downtown with the same goal each time—be more like Jesus than you were the last time. But each time I came to realize that this "no sin" standard was tough business, even after asking myself some good questions that could aid me in my efforts to be more like him. Questions like, what will I need to do to be better prepared this time? And, what sidedoor of my heart will Satan try to enter and how can I lock it before he gets there? While this self-interrogation exercise was helpful, it was by no means a failsafe method in fending off the devil.

And then there's church-league basketball. After four years of not competing due to back and neck surgeries in the late 90s, I returned to the court. Two weeks into the season, my body was doing fine. It was my heart that needed massaged. With everything from keeping track of how many points I scored, to why the stupid referee missed a foul on the shot I also missed, it was much more about repentance than roundball for me. After every game, I spent some time analyzing where my heart and spiritual focus had been during the competition, then made it my goal to show growth in any area of weakness during the next game. While I could never guarantee anyone how my court skills would be displayed on any given night, I could tell them that after the game I would be rebounding from that repentance thing once again.

Then there's the daily battle of driving and the devil riding in the passenger seat. Getting behind the wheel of my vehicle has to be one of the biggest ways my true inner issues come to the surface. Whether it's in regard to the idiot who's following too close, the ignoramus who's driving too fast or the imbecile in the front car at the stoplight who can't seem to find the accelerator when the light turns green, my behavior is often irrational. What's the big deal anyway? As if I've never given a hint to a fellow driver with a near kiss to their bumper. As if I've never acted as though I'm in a time-trial for the next NASCAR race when I'm late for an appointment. As if I've never heard a honk or two from behind when my daydreaming causes a three-second delay in recognizing the light is no longer red. Sin!

Finally, we have to talk about one of my favorite pastimes, watching sports. I've discovered Satan loves watching, too. When my team is being broadcast, back off! Don't you dare walk in front of the television and block my view. I don't care if it's during a huddle, that's my team's huddle. And definitely don't be rooting for the wrong team. You have a television in your own home and nobody will be bothering you there. And don't be criticizing my quarterback. I'm the only one who can criticize my team. And Mr. Referee, you're clearly in danger of the fires of hell due to that horrible call you just made, and God will get his revenge in the end. So silly. So sinful. And I keep telling myself that it's just a game. None of this really matters anyway, right? Even if my team loses by twenty, God will use that loss to humble the players and maybe they'll turn to him, right? It just doesn't matter. Then why does it matter so much to me. Sin!

So watch yourself! Whether you're traveling to the game, watching the game, parking cars at the game, playing in the game or couldn't care less about the game, Satan and his demons are in the game. They entered the contest when you were thrust from your mother's womb, and they've been following you ever since.

Satan also entered the game of one young man more than two-thousand years ago. And for thirty-three years, the man we simply call Jesus didn't make a single error or miss a single shot. Not even once.

*God made him who had
no sin to be sin for us.*

–2 Corinthians 5:21

*The Lord has laid on him
the iniquity of us all.*

–Isaiah 53:6

CHAPTER TWENTY-ONE

The Dark Side

Though Jesus had totally rebelled against every demonic pleading to lust or lose his virginity, on this day sexual deviation enveloped his flesh.

Though loving God had never been relegated to second place or below on his list of priorities, on this day idolatry captivated his mind and cleared his schedule of any thoughts of joyfully submitting to a higher power.

Though thankfulness was as natural to Jesus as waking up, on this day ingratitude and "I deserve this anyway" were his natural responses to the blessings of God.

Though he had welcomed every opportunity to elevate others above himself and leave the best seats open for anybody else but him, on this day he fought to gain an inch to move closer to the front and demanded backstage passes.

Though the desire for attention and acceptance had been tucked away in his humble heart for thirty-three years, on this day he gloried in the masses who witnessed his wonderful words and deeds and basked in the security coming from their admiration and applause.

Though he had carefully walked the narrow road of righteousness and courageously avoided every sinful ditch and devilish detour, on this day he looked for worldly ease and comfort and chose the eight-lane highway with high-volume traffic.

Though he had always been content with leftovers, hand-me-downs and open-air nightly accommodations, on this day he expected prime rib from a personal chef, tailored Ralph Lauren and a presidential suite on the Riviera beachfront.

Though Jesus had lived a life of simplicity and often taught about the dangers of greed, on this day he was all about building bigger barns and selfishly seeking the life of eat, drink and be merry.

Though he had always made it a point to steer far away from any type of debauchery, on this day he was the party animal with no concern about how he acted or whom he might have hurt.

Though he had always cast every temptation of hatred and revenge into the eternal abyss, on this day he pulled the pin from the grenade called bitterness, blowing it up in the face of anyone who had wronged him or worked to make his life more difficult.

Though he had always kept his anger under complete control, on this day he cursed his enemies for their refusal to follow him and made obscene gestures to any who stood in his way of progress.

On this day, Jesus judged a young man solely by the color of his skin and stereotyped him out of a fair future.

On this day, Jesus completely lost his cool and slammed the back of his hand onto the cheek of a helpless three-year-old.

On this day, he cut corners and sought out shortcuts to success.

On this day, he brought his mother to tears with a dishonorable tone.

On this day, he stood his father down and labeled him a loser.

On this day, he divorced his wife because he found someone more satisfying.

On this day, he made prayer secondary.

On this day, he chose sentimentality over standing firm.

On this day, he made a foolish vow.

On this day, he broke a sacred vow.

On this day, he lied about his background on a job application.

On this day, he sentenced someone to prison who was clearly innocent.

On this day, he made fun of an overweight person.

On this day, he whined and complained.

On this day, he demanded.

On this day, he schemed.

On this day, he mocked.

On this day, he manipulated.

On this day, he masterminded the perfect crime.

On this day, he murdered.

On this day, he pretended not to see the starving child holding out their hand for help.

On this day, he came to the clinic and allowed a doctor to end the life of an unborn child God was forming.

On this day, he came to church to work off the guilt from the immorality he had committed the night before.

On this day, he decided not to go to church because he had more important things to do with his time.

On this day, he stood behind the pulpit and preached to gain popularity.

On this day, he used racial slurs to describe a fellow human being.

On this day, he selfishly started a war.

On this day, he arrogantly refused to sign a peace treaty.

On this day, he marched millions of Jews to their appointed deaths in the gas chambers.

On this day, he ordered the slaughter of millions of people in Cambodia.

On this day, he killed thousands of people by flying a commercial jetliner into the World Trade Center.

On this day, he walked into a crowded supermarket with explosives strapped to his body and blew up dozens of unsuspecting shoppers.

Now it's clear from Scriptures that Jesus never actually participated in any of these sins and atrocities. But as God looked down from heaven on the cross and doled out the punishment for your sins, my sins and the sins of the entire world, it was as though Jesus had committed all of them and God was making him pay dearly for it.

It was on that day when Jesus carried our sins to the cross for their rightful punishment. But what's even more amazing is this—as Jesus carried our dark side to the cross and then allowed himself to be fastened with nails to that cross, he himself refused to participate in darkness down to his final breath. If Jesus were ever going to succumb to sin and delight in the dark side, that would have been the ideal time. If he were ever to feel justified in fighting back and seeking some revenge, that would have been the moment to do it.

They falsely accused him. He didn't answer back.

They unfairly convicted him. He didn't demand a new trial.

They laughed at him. He prayed for them.

They called him names. He called on the Father.

They cursed him. He blessed them.

They beat him with their fists again and again. He entrusted himself to God again and again.

They spat on him. He spared them.

They violently whipped him. He silently suffered.

They placed a crown of thorns on his head. He remained a rose.

They pounded nails through his hands and feet. He fought back with mercy, saying *"Father, forgive them, they do not know what they are doing."*

They looked for more hurtful things to say to ridicule him in his final hours. He looked for more hurting people to save.

They did the worst thing man had ever done to God. He did the greatest thing man had ever done for God.

Satan and the forces of evil were taking their best shot at Jesus, but never did they convince him to change allegiance. He was God's man all the way, but still the dark side had to be overcome and the cross was the only way to win this war against a powerful foe. So the one who had never sinned was now volunteering to accept in his flesh the full wrath of God. It was punishment time.

What was it like for Jesus to die on a cross? How did the guilt of sin taste on that day? How did it feel for him to incur the wrath of God for all the sin man had ever committed and would continue to commit in the centuries to come? How was it for Jesus when he became the sacrificial lamb of God to take away your sin?

Have you made any time in your schedule to at least try to understand the intensity of that day?

Do you try to teach others the significance of that day?

Does it bother you that so many seem so casual about what happened to Jesus that day?

Does it ever bring you to tears that billions of people today don't even have a clue about what happened that day?

How much of your life in the past few weeks has been motivated by what happened that day?

Yet that day was the most significant day of your life. It was a very good day indeed. Because it was on that day when every last one of your sins was fastened to the flesh of Jesus. Can you believe it? God took your dark side and gave it to Jesus. And in one, never-seen-before meeting of divine love and justice, Jesus donned the dark side, defeated the dark side, demonstrated his hatred for the dark side and emphatically declared that he would go to any length to remove the dark side in all of us.

"But he was pierced for our transgressions, he was crushed for our iniquities; the punishment that brought us peace was upon him, and by his wounds we are healed" (**Isaiah 53:5**).

The cross of Jesus must always be the central focus of Christianity. Its bearer, its horror, its meaning, its eternal implication for every man and woman and its selfless glory must never be diminished. The stunning truths of the cross must remain in our minds, in our hearts and in our conversations with those we are trying to lead to God.

The cross must serve as the constant reminder of our complete inability and unworthiness to approach God in our own way or based upon our own merits. The cross emphatically states that we will never be acceptable to God because of our good works, our great desires or our grand promises that we'll be better people from now on. Only by the gift of forgiveness, coming through faith in the blood of Jesus, can we be saved from God's wrath in regard to our sin. We don't attain salvation by our moral standards or good works. We obtain salvation by our acceptance of God's grace. This is God's one and only offer. Our acceptance of this offer begins first and foremost with humility. We must come to a crystal clear understanding and a quick admission about who we are in God's sight and what our sin has done to separate ourselves from him. We must humbly admit what we have done to Jesus and why our only remaining hope for a relationship with God hinges on our willingness to be washed clean by his blood (**Titus 3:3-7**). While humility is the key in beginning a relationship with God, it is also essential in the middle, in the end and at all points in between.

May the death of Jesus be the one truth we never forget. May it be the one truth we are proudest to proclaim. And may it be the one truth we cling to more than anything else to help us realize our immense value in the eyes of God.

Then he said to Thomas, "Put your finger here, see my hands. Reach out your hand and put it into my side. Stop doubting and believe." Thomas said to him, "My Lord and my God!"

—John 20:27-28

CHAPTER TWENTY-TWO

My Lord and My God

Just like Thomas, I find it hard at times to embrace the believing part without the seeing part. But why would Thomas have been surprised that Jesus had risen from the dead? Actually, why should anybody (self included) be surprised to hear such unbelievable yet wonderful news? And why should anybody have difficulty believing it? Nothing about Jesus was normal or ordinary from the beginning of his life, so why would we expect anything to be different at the end?

What did it matter that this resurrection miracle had never been witnessed prior to Jesus? Nobody had ever walked on water, made wine from water or calmed the water, but Jesus had already performed that liquid trifecta.

What did it matter that this "coming back to life" claim was medically impossible? It was medically impossible to make leprosy disappear and repair severed spinal cords, but Jesus didn't seem to have any problem with either of those.

What did it matter that there were Roman guards stationed at the tomb to prevent Jesus from exiting if he were somehow able to resurrect? That would be of no concern to him. If Jesus could wake up those who had been dead without any difficulty, couldn't he turn the tables and put to sleep those who had been put in charge of watching his grave?

What did it matter that there was a huge stone covering the entrance to his tomb? Hadn't Jesus gotten himself out of a number of impossible predicaments before this? And couldn't the creator of stones be smart enough to know how to move it, or perhaps turn it into a pebble or a person?

As amazing as it us to us, the resurrection was merely another day at the office or casual walk in the park for Jesus. It is simply one more truth about Jesus that separates him from any possible competition as to whom we should choose to honor and obey as our final authority (**Mathew 28:16-20**). His birth. His fulfillment of specific prophecies. His miracles. His teachings. His love. His perfection. His death. And now, his resurrection!

Buddha, Confucius, Mohammad and many others throughout the centuries have claimed to be God's messengers. Today, billion still cling to the teachings of these men from Earth, but they know little or nothing about the man from heaven. How foolish! How sad! None of those men ever said they would resurrect from the dead. And since it was clearly a non-issue to them, none of them even bothered to determine how they would go about proving it when it happened. And check it out with any of the current followers in those religious groups—none of them will gladly give their lives to tell the world that their leader has risen from the dead. Yet Jesus truly conquered death and was totally unaffected by its lasting sting (**1 Corinthians 15:50-57**).

While Jesus was alive, he wasn't apprehensive or insecure about stating any of it as an already done deal. And when finally put to death and given the opportunity to prove he wasn't just all talk, Jesus walked out of the tomb within three days and accomplished this incredible feat. In regard to his resurrection, let's consider four truths to help us in our understanding of this most unbelievable achievement.

He predicted it

Talk about pressure! Over and over again, Jesus told his twelve apostles and many others that physical death would not signal the end of his life or his ministry (**Luke 9:21-22**). More often than not, his listeners failed to understand that message in its entirety, or perhaps they blew it off as merely metaphorical or more than they could handle at the time. Nevertheless, Jesus continued to predict it. He wanted people to hear it. He hoped they would write it down and then wait for it to happen. He looked forward to his critics trying to make sure it would never happen.

He knew he had come from God and was returning to God (**John 13:3**) and that the tomb was just a temporary stop. Three days would be enough rest for Jesus. Then he would get right back to being for the lost world what they still needed him to be—both Lord and Christ (**Acts 2:36**).

He performed it

Then he did it! Early that Sunday morning, life and breath were given back to the crucified Son of God. His brain waves began to function. His heart started beating. His eyelids were opened. His muscles flexed. His blood flowed. He woke up, sat up, stood up and removed his temporary grave clothes. Then, as a company of Roman soldiers shook with fear and froze as though dead, an angel who would make Mr. Universe look like a lightweight rolled the tremendous stone away from the tomb's entrance and Jesus walked out, never to die again (**Matthew 28:2-4**).

He proved it

Now it was time to show his face. He knew many people would still wonder if it were true, even after seeing him alive. For Jesus, it was all about leaving convincing proof. He didn't want anyone who saw him beyond the grave to think he was only a mirage or a make-pretend friend. He was the same Jesus they had always known, and now he was back from the dead. And he needed to convince more than just a few people. So for forty days, Jesus proved his resurrection was for real. People touched him and talked to him. A privileged few ate with him and were taught by him. Some even received a rebuke from him for their lack of faith as he showed them his crucifixion scars.

Jesus appeared a number of times to different numbers of people. Mary Magdalene was the first to witness his resurrection (**Mark 16:9**). He also had an extended conversation with two disciples somewhere on the way to the town of Emmaus (**Luke 24:13-35**). On another occasion, Jesus had a meal on the beach with seven of his disciples (**John 21:1-14**). He met once with all the apostles except Thomas (**John 20:19-25**), he enjoyed regular fellowship with the remaining eleven apostles (with Thomas in attendance) and met with five-hundred followers on another occasion (**Acts 1:1-9, 1 Corinthians 15:6**).

His visits were well calculated in anticipation of the doubters who lived then and those who remain skeptical today. What if Mary's resurrection claim wasn't taken seriously because most people perceived her to be emotionally distraught and simply in need of more time to move beyond the denial stage of losing a close friend? Perhaps a similar sighting from two trusted people who spent much of an entire day with the risen Jesus would carry more clout with the unbelievers. If that still wasn't enough proof for some, maybe it would help to have a resurrection rally highlighted by personal sharing from seven once-frightened disciples talking about the time they sat around the campfire eating fish and bread with a supposed dead man. Perhaps then this resurrection rumor would establish some credibility. If that were still being concluded as insufficient evidence for the skeptics, could a "he's alive" talk with Thomas put some of their unbelief to death? After all, Thomas was well known amongst his peers for his skepticism about almost everything. Maybe a "touching" testimony from his lips would soften their hearts. What if all that evidence was still judged to be incomplete and unreliable? Could five-hundred people telling their exact same stories about the day they saw Jesus alive help the cause? By this time, the resurrection message would have gained tremendous momentum and been deemed worthy of serious contemplation and investigation.

He preached it

Letting a little more than five-hundred people in on the most important truth of all time was not the plan of Jesus. He wanted everybody to know it and called for the truth of his resurrection to be the cornerstone of his apostles' teaching. So he met with them on numerous occasions and methodically explained this all-important truth from the Scriptures (**Luke 24:44-49, Acts 1:1-9**). He rebuked them for their lack of faith that he would be resurrected, and he charged them to let the world know what they had been privileged to witness (**Mark 16:14-16**). For forty days, he trained them for their mission. For forty days, his physical presence eroded any of their lingering doubts. For forty days, he listened as the apostles asked their questions. For forty days, he pleaded with them to preach about the answers he supplied. And for forty days, he encouraged them to cling to the joy of his resurrection and the certainty of theirs to come.

These apostles were the lifeline of salvation to all men and women from that day forward. And from what we read documented in the book of Acts and confirmed in the epistles (**Colossians 1:23**), and from the billions who have clung tightly to this resurrection truth since the first century, they were truly successful in their mission to both humbly and proudly convey that Jesus had indeed conquered death. And today, we are the beneficiaries of their boldness.

The resurrection of Jesus is an historical fact. Should we be shocked by that? Should we be surprised? Should we hold out hope that it happened, or have complete confidence? Should we doubt it, or fully disclose it? After watching and listening to an amazing presentation of talent in the life of Jesus, doesn't his encore seem to fit? And if the fireworks display has made you ooh and aah, shouldn't the finale leave you breathless?

See to it that no one takes you captive through hollow and deceptive philosophy, which depends on human tradition and the basic principles of this world rather than on Christ.

–Colossians 2:8

CHAPTER TWENTY-THREE

More About the Messiah

By no means was Satan finished with Jesus. He had failed on every front in his efforts to sabotage God's plan, and he was outraged. Every attempt he had made to convince Jesus to sell out to shortcuts or succumb to sin had been thoroughly rejected. And he couldn't deny that the power Jesus possessed had completely overshadowed his. He knew the many miracles Jesus performed were still fresh on the minds of those who saw them, and that recipients of those miracles were still around to relay their stories. What once looked like a huge victory for his side as Jesus hung in shame on a Roman crucifix was now just another sore spot and sour reminder of his own futility. The triumph and true meaning of the cross was making a public spectacle of him and his defeated troops (**Colossians 2:13-15**). Rubbing salt into his already painful wound, the resurrection exposed a fatal flaw in his fear and intimidation tactics regarding physical death (**Hebrews 2:14-16**). But Satan still had life and permission to roam the Earth. Filled with fury, there was still much work to be done by the leader of the dark side (**Revelation 12:12**).

Though he was unable to attack Jesus in the flesh upon his ascension to heaven, Satan quickly shifted his primary focus on deceiving to the followers of Jesus, all those who were courageously spreading the message of his perfect life, his purposeful death and his powerful resurrection (**1 Peter 5:8-9, Revelation 12:7-13**). The devil's goal was simple—keep people from receiving the forgiveness of their sins and distract them from finding their way to the perfect place from where he had been eternally exiled.

Now that Jesus was no longer visible to the human eye, Satan counted on mankind to become more open to his lies and half-truths. He believed his deceit could be used to derail them on their journey to salvation. Jesus wasn't around anymore to answer the all-important questions about God and how to please him. And he wasn't there to pop a miracle in their presence and reestablish his rightful claim of being God's final statement to the world. So Satan set out to do what he has always done better than anyone—lie (**John 8:42-44**).

But God was one step ahead of him. First, the Old Testament truths concerning Jesus were becoming more available to the common man. Along with that, the message of Jesus was going forth rapidly by word of mouth from those who knew him best. And within a few decades, people were discovering and rediscovering more amazing truths about Jesus in the letters from Romans to Revelation, as well as in the book of Acts and the four Gospels that would be coming soon—much-needed information that was being circulated to every church and every disciple in the first century. These letters and biographies of Jesus were essential for the continued growth of Christianity and to counter Satan's lies. God's plan was to use these powerful reminders of Jesus to blow away any dark clouds or dense fog that may have settled in the minds of believers or potential believers. Much false teaching and demonic misdirection were available for consumption, so God was making sure the truths of Jesus could live on, even though he was no longer there.

Praise God we still have access to these same documents. So since we've already taken a closer look at Jesus in the four Gospels, let's consider some of the affirmations and reaffirmations found in the remainder of the New Testament that will help to keep us on the straight and narrow road in regard to our understanding of him. These were the same reminders that helped to solidify the faith of our first-century brothers and sisters in the midst of the many lies being told to them.

When initially presented, these eternal truths rattled the cages of doubting disciples and unbelievers both. When accepted, they provided the key to escape. And these truths are meant to do the same for us two-thousand years later. Jesus is still the same now as he was then. Nothing about him has changed, and nothing ever will.

Regardless of the outright lies and half-truths you and I may hear about Jesus today, the whole truth is still obvious. Is Jesus just another prophet in the company of Moses and Elijah? Is he merely a mighty angel rather than the mighty God? Is he just a great teacher, one of many whom God has used over the years to inform people of the deeper meaning of love and good will? Was his death on a cross a sign of weakness and defeat, or one of strength and victory? Did Jesus fail in his first mission to set up his kingdom so one day in the future he'll make another run at it?

Many of these questions about Jesus are still eliciting wrong responses. Yet all can be answered in the information left in these letters, boldly written with the perfect aid and oversight of the Holy Spirit. They will remind us that Jesus was indeed all God and all man, and that eternal life is found only in him and through him. Here's a small sampling of "Jesus truths" from these writings.

Lord and Messiah
The Holy and Righteous One
The Author of Life
Prince and Savior
Lord of All
As to his human nature, a descendant of David
He was declared with power to be the Son of God
At the right hand of God and is also interceding for us
God over all, forever praised
The end of the Law
The Lord of both the living and the dead
Christ is the power of God and the wisdom of God
Our Passover lamb
The image of God
Who gave himself for our sins to rescue us from the present evil age

In him we have redemption through his blood, the forgiveness of sins

For he himself is our peace

Christ Jesus the cornerstone

The head of the church

Christ Jesus, who being in very nature God, did not consider equality with God something to be grasped

Therefore God exalted him to the highest place and gave him the name that is above every name

He is the image of the invisible God

For by him all things were created

He is before all things, and in him all things hold together

He is the beginning and the firstborn from among the dead, so that in everything he might have the supremacy

For God was pleased to have all his fullness dwell in him

The mystery of God, in whom are hidden all the treasures of wisdom and knowledge

In Christ all the fullness of Deity lives in bodily form

The head over every power and authority

The reality, however, is found in Christ

Christ is all, and is in all

Christ Jesus, who has destroyed death

Christ Jesus, who will judge the living and the dead

Heir of all things

The radiance of God's glory and the exact representation of his being

A merciful and faithful high priest in service to God

Worthy of greater honor than Moses

Such a high priest meets our needs—one who is holy, blameless, pure, set apart from sinners, exalted above the heavens

The Author and Perfector of our faith

The Great Shepherd of the sheep

Jesus Christ, our only Sovereign and Lord

The only God our Savior be glory, majesty, power and authority, Jesus Christ our Lord

The Word of Life

The Life

The First and the Last

He holds the keys of death and Hades
The Lion of the tribe of Judah
Lord of lords and King of kings
The Bright Morning Star

Since the first century, the greatness and supremacy of Jesus have withstood numerous attempts by Satan and his evil empire to either be fully forgotten or brought down to a less-lofty status. Many leaders of the Roman Empire made efforts to snuff out Christianity by snuffing out individual Christians, and they often made them suffer intensely until their final breaths could be taken. But the glory of Jesus continued to be revealed by each of those martyr's refusal to call him anything but Lord, even after being offered amnesty for a simple, one-time denial of their faith. The Roman emperor Nero accused Jesus' followers of arson when fire broke out in the great city. They claimed the only fire they were responsible for spreading was the message of salvation, due to the Holy Spirit who burned within them. Later, the emperor Domitian demanded that every resident of Rome recognize him as deity. The disciples stood their ground and claimed that Jesus was the only one they would ever refer to as God.

When it was finally concluded that the church of Jesus couldn't be stamped out and defeated, and that persecution against its members seemed to be promoting their growth instead, Satan offered up a new plan of attack and Christianity became the state religion of Rome in the early fourth century. But true disciples who were well aware of Satan's schemes refused to accept the compromised, watered-down version of Christianity that was being promoted by the majority and clung tightly to the eternal truths of Jesus.

Throughout the past two-thousand years, the magnificence of Jesus has survived the many wars that have been falsely fought in his name, the inability to mass-produce printed documents revealing his true credentials, the criticisms of liberal scholars, the low number of true Christians at different stages of history and the high numbers of false teachers at other times. Today's attempts in movies, mini-series and magazine articles to discount the man, the message he brought and the majesty he rightly possesses haven't changed the truths you just read about in this chapter or in this entire book. Today's religious movements that say Jesus is powerful but not perfect, or delightful but not deity, are misleading lost souls and keeping them from an opportunity to meet the real deal in heaven one day. And churches that tell the truth about who Jesus is but don't expect people to put all of his teachings into practice are sending an equally damning message to those attending their gatherings.

Oh that all mankind might come to know more about Jesus and give him the appropriate worship and discipleship that he so richly deserves. And let it begin with me!

*Since the children have flesh and blood,
he too shared in their humanity...*

—Hebrews 2:14

CHAPTER TWENTY-FOUR

Jesus in Blue Jeans

Imagine for a moment you had received a message from Jesus saying he was going to drop by your home in a few days, spend a little time with you and have a chat. How would you prepare for an event of that magnitude? What would you do for the next few days to get yourself and your home ready for a visit from the Son of God.

Now, compared to other worries you will likely have about that visit, what I'm about to say will seem quite trivial. But one of the decisions you'll have to make involves what you'll be wearing that day. Would you feel the need to go purchase some new and improved threads, bypassing the selection currently hanging in your closet? Will you dress up, go casual or land somewhere in the middle? But before you make your final decision, you should probably ask yourself another question: What will Jesus be wearing? And if he's dressed up and you're not, oh no! And if he comes casual and you're in a dress or a coat and tie, oh no again!

Relax! My guess is Jesus would come to your house, my house and the White House wearing blue jeans. It makes complete sense to me. After all, doesn't everybody wear blue jeans? Rich people, poor people, middle-class people. Young people, old people, middle-aged people. Black people, White people, Asian people, Native-American people, Latin-American people. CEO's and cement truck drivers wear blue jeans. Doctors and ditch diggers wear blue jeans. Heads of state and the homeless wear blue jeans. Professional athletes and part-time hot dog vendors wear blue jeans.

Now I'm not sure if Gap, Tommy Hilfiger, Wrangler, Lee or Levi would be his brand of choice. And I'm not sure if he'd wear relaxed fit, straight leg, baggy or boot cut (maybe carpenter jeans). But in my opinion, Jesus would come to your place wearing blue jeans. He wants you to feel secure and at ease. He wants to relate to you. He wants to be as approachable as possible. And although he is who he is, he's never desired to flaunt it or throw it in your face. He's always been fine with being just one of the gang, and he's never seemed to have a problem in that setting. So a few minutes before his planned arrival, put on your favorite pair of blue jeans, pour a couple glasses of iced-tea and plop yourself down on your couch. Just don't forget to answer the door when he comes. Jesus has never been the kind to barge in without knocking or knowing he's welcome (**Revelation 3:19-20**).

Now that your choice of clothing is no longer bringing on anxiety, you should ask yourself a question that's much more important than the one about your outer covering. What do you suppose Jesus will want to discuss with you? What information will he be seeking to uncover? What questions will he ask you and in which direction will the conversation turn? What topic will be first? And what will interest him the most about you? Will it be your trophy collection, or maybe your stock portfolio? Sure, Jesus would be interested in hearing about your athletic endeavors, but wouldn't he be more concerned with how you're competing against your sinful nature? And sure, he'd probably check to see where your investments are heading, but wouldn't he care a lot more about where you're investing your time and energy?

And what would Jesus try to change in your life? Will your furniture or favorite team become a topic for change? Probably not! More than likely, Jesus would sit on anything, cheer for anybody and welcome you to join him in both. Will your job or savings account balance make it into the conversation about change? Maybe. But Jesus would be happy if you're gainfully employed, and as far as your finances were concerned, he'd remind you that the money in your account should never relate to the joy in your life, whether that's a little or a lot. What about your hobbies, your choice of vehicle or your upcoming vacation plans? Would these things really matter that much to Jesus? I'm sure he would be interested in hearing about all of those. But from what I've found in the Scriptures, let me propose to you four areas in your life that I believe Jesus would look to change during his one-on-one time with you.

First, Jesus will try to change your *self-esteem*. More than anything else, he will want you to know that you're deeply loved. He will want you to gain great security from that love, and he'll undoubtedly want you to feel special and unique, a one-and-only "I made you to be you" creation of God.

Unfortunately, most of us don't feel very good about who we are. Things happened early on in our lives (and are still happening) that convinced us we're "has-beens" or "never-will-be's." Perhaps we gained those beliefs from our parents, our peers, our failures, our looks or lack thereof, our weight (usually too much) or our authority figures. Maybe we heard "that's not good enough" or "you'll never amount to anything" one too many times. Oh, we act like we're important and valuable to society, but most of us don't really believe it's true.

I have a four-inch scar on the right side of my face, there for all the world to see since I was fourteen, coming from an embarrassing and painful rendezvous with barbed-wire. That scar has led to a number of battles with my insecurity, and many times I've come out on the losing end.

My past sins of impurity, sexual immorality, drunkenness, anger, jealousy, selfishness, deceit, pride, prejudice and the many consequences that followed have also been put on my "you're a lost cause" list. It's these and dozens of other reminders of my self-focused and sinful nature that love to visit me during a typical day, often throwing me into the "I'm a failure" pit where God's sign says "No Trespassing."

It's so easy for me to move in the direction of self-condemnation. When I was eighteen, I made a hole-in-one, but I also shot 102 for the round that day. More than one-hundred is great on a history course, but not on a golf course! It's impossible for me to think about that ace in the context of a one-hole accomplishment. Almost every time someone asks me if I've ever made a hole-in-one, I answer in the affirmative but feel compelled to share about the tragedy that occurred on the other seventeen holes.

What are your hang-ups and deepest insecurities? What are the roots of your self-esteem slumps? Many of us probably feel a little like the leper might have felt when Jesus stopped by and sat on his couch one day. Since we don't know his name, let's give him one. Let's call him Lawrence.

Nobody but Lawrence and perhaps a few of his diseased friends had sat on his couch in quite some time. Lawrence was forced by all the smooth-skin people in town to hang a sign on his couch reading "Unclean Upholstery" so normal and important-to-God folks would stay as far away as possible from him so as not to become unclean and unacceptable. So for the longest time, it was just Lawrence and his couch. It was lonely there. And the longer Lawrence sat there all by himself, the more he became convinced he really deserved that fate. Every once in a while Lawrence tried to convince himself he was normal and okay, but when the next fifty people who saw him sitting on his couch hurriedly darted away in disgust, he was once again sure he was wrong. Why, even the priests and teachers of the law never came close to Lawrence's couch, let alone sit on it. So Lawrence concluded God definitely wasn't interested in him.

Then one day, Lawrence saw Jesus coming his way. He had heard some exciting rumors about Jesus and thought perhaps Jesus could perform one of his miracles on him and cure him of his dreaded disease. If so, Lawrence once and for all could be set free from the lonely-couch syndrome. When Lawrence saw Jesus approaching, he rose from his couch and fell at his feet, begging him for a cure. Then something strange happened. Jesus motioned for Lawrence to move back to his couch. But before he had time to think that this most recent hope for a normal life had just been shattered, Lawrence noticed Jesus heading for his couch, looking as though he was about to take a seat there.

Before Lawrence could shout out the expected "Unclean, Unclean," Jesus plopped down on his couch. And for the first time since leprosy had been confirmed by his physician, Lawrence felt hope. Somebody actually cared. Somebody actually thought he wasn't totally useless. Then that somebody did what Lawrence had resigned in his mind would never happen again—he touched him. Not only was Jesus on his couch, which would have made Lawrence's decade, now he was holding his hand, which made his life! Self-esteem was gushing everywhere. The "Old Faithful" geyser of good feeling lying dormant inside of Lawrence was going off for the first time in ages, and she would never shut down. Lawrence probably could have lived on as a leper, now that someone had finally sat on his couch. He could have found joy for quite some time just knowing that at least one person found him worthy of talking-to and touch. The physical cure that followed was incredible and life-changing. But the visitor on his couch and the touch of his hand were what Lawrence really needed. Jesus did for Lawrence what nobody else was willing to do—he loved him and went the second mile to make sure he knew it.

Jesus loves sitting on your couch, too. It isn't important to him how many other people have sat on it so far. He's sitting on it right now and telling you the same thing he told Lawrence: "You're special, you're important, you're valuable and you're loved." But that shouldn't surprise you, should it? It's what Jesus told every person he ever met, whether in words or in the way he treated them.

Now that you've found some much needed self-esteem and security, Jesus would try to *change your thinking.* He'll do that because he knows that much of our knowledge is incomplete. Most of us have relied way too much on what we think, what we feel and what we've been taught. But some of the information we've collected through the years is off. Some of it is probably way off! Jesus just want us to be on—on track and on target, especially in matters pertaining to eternity.

During his well-known Sermon on the Mount, Jesus sat on the couch with a number of disciples and did everything he could to change their way of thinking. The phrase "You have heard it said" was followed up each time with a corrective note of "But I tell you" (**Matthew 5:21-48**). The teaching so many in that era had been exposed to was often old-fashioned, incorrect and, in many cases, just flat wrong. Jesus knew that if those individuals in his hearing continued in their belief of the popular belief, they would miss out on the full life and the eternal home he was promising. Even the twelve apostles Jesus selected to carry on his mission were totally confused on a regular basis, and Jesus spent three years sitting on their couches trying to change their wayward thinking.

So what have you heard? Is it right? Are you open to being wrong? Would you be defensive if Jesus pointed out a major misunderstanding in your belief system? What if he tried to tweak your mind just a bit to help you gain a fuller understanding of an important truth? Could he go anywhere in your brain and scramble things without you pulling the plug on him? Would Jesus find your doctrine to be accurate? Would he offer you a better way of treating people than what you're doing at the moment? Would he have to help you calm down and get a better grip on how God is involved in everything that happens in your life? Would you be willing to pour him another glass of iced-tea and invite him to stay a little longer so more of your incorrect thinking could be discovered? Jesus will stay on your couch only as long as you want him to stay. That's how he operated while walking this planet, and that's how he determines couch-time today.

Now that you're well on your way to a proper understanding of important truths, Jesus will try to *change your eternity*. For Jesus, it was never enough that people knew what was true. Instead, it was always about their acceptance of the truth and how those truths were going to alter their daily lives. More than anything else, Jesus wanted people he met to be saved. His ultimate goal was to make sure he could sit down with them on their heavenly couches and welcome them to their eternal mansions. That's why Jesus came. Eternity and helping people experience it was his ultimate goal.

Jesus would help you discover what might be standing in the way of his hope becoming your reality. Or he would make you aware of what you're too focused on currently that's keeping you from thinking more about eternity. He would elaborate on the fact that "this" life is not "the" life and he would plead with you to put all your eggs in the heavenly basket so they couldn't be broken by the things of the world.

Once Jesus turned your focus to heaven, he would tell you exactly how to get there. He would unfold a treasure map on your coffee table and mark out significant points of interest. He would highlight the roads of faith, repentance, discipleship and baptism. Then he would boldly star the twin cities of loving God and loving your neighbor (**Matthew 22:34-40**). Finally, he would direct you to the great state of humility, outline it and warn you about the grave dangers that lie beyond its borders. Then he would roll up the map, hand it to you and tell you to read it as often as possible.

Before leaving your home, Jesus would address one final area in your life. He would try to *change your purpose.* Jesus would consider it incomplete to secure salvation for someone without calling that person to be an active witness for him and an activist for the poor and less fortunate. These were the very things his followers devoted their energies to in the first century.

In regard to spreading the word about Jesus, the woman at the well got his message and left with the message to convert an entire city (**John 4:27-39**). The demon-possessed man living in the cemetery heeded the call and set off on a ten-city tour telling people about Jesus after his remarkable transformation (**Mark 5:1-20**). The apostles and thousands of others who were converted in the first thirty years of the church gladly accepted the challenge that accompanied their salvation and told the entire world about Jesus (**Acts 17:6, 28:21-22, Colossians 1:23**).

In regard to caring for the poor and needy, the early church accepted it as part of their discipleship. They knew Jesus preached about it often, and many had seen him live it out in their presence (**Luke 14:12-14**). Even if nobody else cared, the poor could always rely on Christians and their leaders to feel their pain and open their pocketbooks (**Galatians 2:8-10**). The sick could count on regular visits, the lame wouldn't be left alone and the prisoners wouldn't be forgotten as long as true disciples roamed the Earth (**Matthew 25:31-46**). Simply put, Jesus would expect you to get off your couch and go searching for those who needed assistance—physical, emotional or spiritual.

Jesus would definitely ask you what you're living for at this stage of your life. He would be saddened if he had to inform you that your talents and energies are mostly being spent on the non-eternal. He would charge you to be making disciples while you're making money. He would remind you to offer the ladder to heaven for your co-workers while you're climbing the ladder to success. He would tell you to get more joy from your children memorizing a difficult Scripture than scoring the game-winning goal, and to congratulate them more enthusiastically for a Bible breakthrough than a buzzer-beater. He would implore you to remember that gaining disciples is your first goal while you're gaining a degree. He would remind you that people are lost and that heaven and hell are real. He would paint graphic pictures of the hidden pain living inside those you know, and then warn you not to be faked out by their smiling exteriors. He would tell you of the amazing joy that will accompany your efforts to fish for him, and the even greater joy that comes when you finally catch someone. He would tell you to make the extra call, take more chances in inviting people to church or to study the Scriptures, even if it means looking foolish, and never assume anybody is going to heaven just because they believe they are.

Jesus would ask you to open your eyes to the many hurting people in the world, not just those who are thousands of miles away in a third-world country, but also those who live in your neck of the woods. He would point you to the closest homeless shelter and halfway house and ask you to try and make a difference with those living there. He would offer you the address of the nearest nursing home and encourage you to go play Bingo with the residents or hold the hand of an Alzheimer's patient. He would remind you about the orphanage in town and ask you to offer some love to a ten-year-old who has never seen it. And he would ask you to drive by the prison more often and think about what the inmates really need and how you might be able to help.

So how have you done on the couch? During this chapter and throughout this entire book, you've been on the couch with Jesus. What have you heard? What have you felt? What have you learned? What have you decided?

Jesus in blue jeans—he has shown himself to be incredibly down-to-earth. He's infinitely kind and completely loving. He's unapologetic about his expectations. And without a doubt, he is persistent. Was he successful in his time with you? Do you know him better now? Do you love him more than you did before this latest visit? What can you tell others about Jesus now that you've had your time on the couch with him?

I'm certain many more books will be written about Jesus in your lifetime. More than likely, you'll read a few of them before your days are done. And you will probably hear a number of sermons that will attempt to uncover his true character and reveal his true glory. Never tire of it. Never think you've had enough. Welcome it. Search out more about Jesus than you think you should. Make it your all-consuming passion to get to know the one who would be wearing blue jeans if he were to meet with you on Earth, and the one who will be wearing a big smile when he meets you in heaven.

But if anyone obeys his word, God's love is truly made complete in him. This is how we know we are in him: Whoever claims to live in him must walk as Jesus did.

–1 John 2:5-6

EPILOGUE

In His Steps

Must—it's a four-letter word that many people have chosen to eliminate from their spiritual vocabularies. We live in a religious world that focuses a whole lot more on admiration than application when it comes to Jesus. It's one thing to admire Jesus. It's a completely different challenge to imitate him. It's one thing to talk about Jesus. It's another thing altogether to walk like him.

"But Jesus was perfect, and I'm certainly never going to be perfect," many would counter defensively. Yes, but God was well aware of that truth when he chose to include this passage in the written word.

"I'm certainly going to try, but you can't expect too much." That's the typical talk heard coming from those whose spiritual thermostats are set on lukewarm.

But the word "try" isn't in the text. As Yoda remarked to a young Luke Skywalker after he had just given up hope of raising a disabled starship from a swamp in *The Empire Strikes Back*—*"Do, or do not; there is no try!"*

We're so caught up in creating our clever excuses for where we are with God today, many of us haven't grown in years in becoming more like Jesus. We're spiritually stuck. And until we develop a conviction that God is serious about this verse being honored and obeyed, our spiritual starships will remain in swamps of religiosity and mediocrity.

It's high time to take the word *must* to heart and get serious about the call to walk in the footsteps of Jesus. If you only know who Jesus is and it ends there, it would be better if the two of you had never been introduced. But after seeing this amazing life, why wouldn't you want to learn how to imitate him? So allow me to bring this book and our journey to an end with some practical thoughts about how to walk in his steps.

First, you'll need to swallow your pride and ask for help. God has designed us to both need help and provide help for each other, and I'm guessing there are at least a few people who would love to help you on this exciting journey (**Hebrews 3:12-14, 10:24-25**). Get all the assistance you possibly can in a one-on-one discipling relationship, but also get involved in some type of small group with people of a similar passion. While Jesus was a master of wowing the huge crowds with his words and wisdom, and while he radically changed a number of lives in one-on-one encounters, most of the training and character building he accomplished with the men who would later change the world was done in a group setting. It's my conviction that in the right atmosphere of "one student telling another student what they're learning in preparation for the final exam," you can experience tremendous spiritual growth in a discipleship group.

Secondly, go at it with passion. Make it your number one focus in life (**2 Timothy 2:1-7**). At different times in my life, I've been willing to subject myself to much sacrifice, pain and humiliation in order to get what I wanted. I worked an entire summer with my college roommate doing nightly cleanup at a slaughterhouse. It was by far the most disgusting job I have ever had. But I needed the extra cash and no other would-be employer was offering me the kind of money I was making there. I also worked for a few years as a city-league basketball referee. My roommate and I needed sufficient funds to support our many sports' addictions, which included a 25-inch color television (top of the line in 1980) to watch all the big events, and season tickets to University of Washington football games. If you don't know anything about city-league basketball, the men you often find playing there are former high-school subs who think they missed a shot at the NBA because of bad timing or unfortunate injuries. They play their hearts out for the five fans in attendance and can't believe you would actually make a call against them. I was told where to go on a number of occasions, and, believe me, it wasn't over to their house for snacks after the game! But I endured the scorn and shame and suffered for the cause of keeping sports at the forefront of my life. If that's how I was willing to live to serve an idol, then certainly I can do at least that much in pursuing Jesus (**Colossians 3:23**).

Third, think of a few people you admire in regard to their ability to imitate Jesus, then carefully observe how they go about it. It's amazing how much we can learn just by watching for a while. Spend some time with those people, ask them questions and elicit their help in your efforts (**1 Corinthians 4:14-17**).

Fourth, read the four Gospel accounts over and over again and keep putting Jesus before your eyes. Much of Christianity is simply relearning what we've already learned but somehow are slow to put into practice. Read through them slowly and think about what you see. Watch Jesus in action in a specific area, then make it your goal that day to imitate him in the exact same way (**2 Peter 1:5-15**).

Next, pray about it every day. What prayer could be more important and more honoring to God than the simple prayer of "God, please help me to be like Jesus?" Don't you think God might be eager to answer that one? Be specific. Be humble. Admit your shortcomings and beg him for wisdom and strength to live up to the name Christian (**Colossians 1:9-13**).

Sixth, get regular reviews. Don't get direction on how to be a better disciple and then find out how you're doing months later. Invite people to be involved in your life consistently. Ask them from time to time to tell you what they see in you that needs to become more like Jesus. Ask them to also tell you about any positive results they've seen and the ways they've noticed you growing and changing. Remember, we are usually not the best judges of whether or not we're being formed into the image of Jesus (**Colossians 1:28-29**).

Next, rest in the grace that's readily available. Certainly don't plan to fail or fall short, but accept his incredibly kind plan called grace when you realize your shortcomings and sins. Enjoy the continual forgiveness and cleansing promised to you as you take the thrilling ride of discipleship, and take pride in the honor of having a role model and rust remover like Jesus (**Romans 5:6-11**).

Finally, don't quit. You can live as a disciple, and you can be a strong one all the days of your life. Satan will tempt you to think that it's just not for you, but that's just not true (**Hebrews 10:32-39**). Keep walking in the footsteps of Jesus and God will honor your determination.

The plan for spiritual growth may not be what you want or expect, and it will include some pain and self-denial along the way. But it will succeed if you submit to it. For some, that plan might involve getting open with a sin that you can't seem to overcome, or telling the whole truth about a sin that is slowly but surely hardening your heart. Or it might involve apologizing to that person you don't really want to apologize to. The plan for you might be to set your alarm an hour earlier than normal so you can spend quality time in prayer and Bible study before leaving for work. Or it might mean you'll need to put a block on your computer so you can't access the pornography that has recently imprisoned you. Perhaps the plan involves a breakup with the person you're dating because you're pulling each other down spiritually. Or it could be about rearranging your financial priorities so you can start honoring the Lord with your wealth. Whatever plan God has for you to be more like Jesus, don't dismiss it. Repentance is a tough step, but times of refreshing are waiting on the other side (**Acts 3:17-20**).

We have absolutely no choice in the matter of who Jesus is and what he has done. It's history, and a remarkable history at that. We do have a choice, however, about how we're going to respond to what we have seen and heard. Walking in his steps is the only choice which will provide you with the abundant life now and ensure you that one day you will hear those wonderful words of Jesus as you stand on the doorstep of heaven: *"Well done, good and faithful servant; enter the joy of your Master."*

If this book has helped you resist the urge to be unimpressed with Jesus, praise God for his power over the dark side and their evil plans to minimize his greatness. If this book has helped you replace despair with hope for a full life, praise God for his power over your discouragement and decision to settle for less. If this book has helped you discover another peak in your spiritual climb, praise God for his power over your plateaus. And if this book has helped you notice the enemy in your rear-view mirror, praise God for his power over the devil's plan to run you off the narrow road and keep you from your final destination.

I often hear believers say that if there were ever a time when the world needed to hear from Jesus, it's now. I've said it myself on occasion. But I suppose anybody who has ever embraced his message or claimed allegiance to him could have uttered that same statement regarding the times in which they lived. Truth be told, there has never been a time in the past two-thousand years when the words of Jesus weren't in urgent need of being heard and followed.

I hope this book about Jesus has encouraged you to speak about him more courageously and inspired you to follow him more closely. Our world is definitely in need of more men and women doing both!

Books for Christian Growth at www.ipibooks.com

Apologetics

Compelling Evidence for God and the Bible—Truth in an Age of Doubt, by Douglas Jacoby.
Field Manual for Christian Apologetics, by John M. Oakes.
Is There A God—Questions and Answers about Science and the Bible, by John M. Oakes.
Mormonism—What Do the Evidence and Testimony Reveal?, by John M. Oakes.
Reasons For Belief-A Handbook of Christian Evidence, by John M. Oakes.
That You May Believe—Reflections on Science and Jesus, by John Oakes/David Eastman.
The Resurrection: A Historical Analysis, by C. Foster Stanback.
When God Is Silent—The Problem of Human Suffering, by Douglas Jacoby.

Bible Basics

A Disciple's Handbook—Third Edition, Tom A. Jones, Editor.
A Quick Overview of the Bible, by Douglas Jacoby.
Be Still, My Soul—A Practical Guide to a Deeper Relationship with God, by Sam Laing.
From Shadow to Reality—Relationship of the Old & New Testament, by John M. Oakes.
Getting the Most from the Bible, Second Edition, by G. Steve Kinnard.
Letters to New Disciples—Practical Advice for New Followers of Jesus, by Tom A. Jones.
The Baptized Life—The Lifelong Meaning of Immersion into Christ, by Tom A. Jones.
The Lion Never Sleeps—Preparing Those You Love for Satans Attacks, by Mike Taliaferro.
The New Christian's Field Guide, Joseph Dindinger, Editor.
Thirty Days at the Foot of the Cross, Tom and Sheila Jones, Editors.
The Spirit—Presense & Power, Sense & Nonsense, by Douglas Jacoby.

Christian Living

According to Your Faith—The Awesome Power of Belief in God, by Richard Alawaye.
But What About Your Anger—A Biblical Guide to Managing Your Anger, by Lee Boger.
Caring Beyond the Margins—Understanding Homosexuality, by Guy Hammond.
Golden Rule Membership—What God Expects of Every Disciple, by John M. Oakes.
How to Defeat Temptation in Under 60 Seconds, by Guy Hammond.
Jesus and the Poor—Embracing the Ministry of Jesus, by G. Steve Kinnard.
How to Be a Missionary in Your Hometown, by Joel Nagel.
Like a Tree Planted by Streams of Water—Personal Spiritual Growth, G. Steve Kinnard.
Love One Another—Importance & Power of Christian Relationships, by Gordon Ferguson.
One Another—Transformational Relationships, by Tom A. Jones and Steve Brown.
Prepared to Answer—Restoring Truth in An Age of Relativism, by Gordon Ferguson.
Repentance—A Cosmic Shift of Mind & Heart, by Edward J. Anton.
Strong in the Grace—Reclaiming the Heart of the Gospel, by Tom A. Jones.
The Guilty Soul's Guide to Grace—Freedom in Christ, by Sam Laing.
The Power of Discipling, by Gordon Ferguson.
The Prideful Soul's Guide to Humility, by Tom A. Jones and Michael Fontenot.
The Way of the Heart—Spiritual Living in a Legalistic World, by G. Steve Kinnard.
The Way of the Heart of Jesus—Prayer, Fasting, Bible Study, by G. Steve Kinnard.
Till the Nets Are Full—An Evangelism Handbook for the 21st Century, by Douglas Jacoby.
Thrive—Using Psalms to Help You Flourish, by Douglas Jacoby.
Walking the Way of the Heart—Lessons for Spiritual Living, by G. Steve Kinnard.
What Happens After We Die?, by Douglas Jacoby.
What Now, God? Finding God in Transitions, by Jeanie Shaw.
When God is Silent—The Problem of Human Suffering, by Douglas Jacoby.
Values and Habits of Spiritual Growth, by Bryan Gray.

Deeper Study

A Women's Ministry Handbook, by Jennifer Lambert and Kay McKean.
After The Storm—Hope & Healing From Ezra—Nehemiah, by Rolan Dia Monje.
Aliens and Strangers—The Life and Letters of Peter, by Brett Kreider.
Crossing the Line: Culture, Race, and Kingdom, by Michael Burns.
Daniel—Prophet to the Nations, by John M. Oakes.
Exodus—Making Israel's Journey Your Own, by Rolan Dia Monje.
Exodus—Night of Redemption, by Douglas Jacoby.
Finish Strong—The Message of Haggai, Zechariah, and Malachi, by Rolan Dia Monje.
Free Your Mind—40 Days to Greater Peace, Hope, and Joy, by Sam Laing.
In Remembrance of Me—Understanding the Lord's Supper, by Andrew C. Fleming.
In the Middle of It!—Tools to Help Preteen and Young Teens, by Jeff Rorabaugh.
Into the Psalms—Verses for the Heart, Music for the Soul, by Rolan Dia Monje.
King Jesus—A Survey of the Life of Jesus the Messiah, by G. Steve Kinnard.
Jesus Unequaled—An Exposition of Colossians, by G. Steve Kinnard.
Mornings in Matthew, by Tammy Fleming.
Passport to the Land of Enough—Revised Edition, by Joel Nagel.
Prophets I—The Voices of Yahweh, by G. Steve Kinnard.
Prophets II—The Prophets of the Assyrian Period, by G. Steve Kinnard.
Prophets III—The Prophets of the Babylonian and Persion Periods, by G. Steve Kinnard.
Return to Sender—When There's Nowhere Left to God but Home, by Guy Hammond.
Romans—The Heart Set Free, by Gordon Ferguson.
Revelation Revealed—Keys to Unlocking the Mysteries of Revelation, by Gordon Ferguson.
Spiritual Leadership for Women, Jeanie Shaw, Editor.
The Call of the Wise—An Introduction and Index of Proverbs, by G. Steve Kinnard.
The Cross of the Savior—From the Perspective of Jesus..., by Mark Templer.
The Final Act—A Biblical Look at End-Time Prophecy, by G. Steve Kinnard.
The Gospel of Matthew—The Crowning of the King, by G. Steve Kinnard.
The King Jesus Translation of the New Testament, by G. Steve Kinnard.
The Letters of James, Peter, John, Jude—Life to the Full, by Douglas Jacoby.
The Lion Has Roared—An Exposition of Amos, by Douglas Jacoby.
The Mission—God and Make Disciples of All Nations, by Will and Kristen Lambert
The Recovery Journal—Jesus' Heart to Help the Hurting, by Timothy Sumerlin.
The Seven People Who Help You to Heaven, by Sam Laing.
Wildfire—How Progressive Theology is Impacting the Church, by Daren Overstreet
World Changers—The History of the Church in the Book of Acts, by Gordon Ferguson.

Marriage and Family

A Lifetime of Love—Building and Growing Your Marriage, by Al and Gloria Baird
Building Emotional Intimacy in Your Marriage, by Jeff and Florence Schachinger.
Hot and Holy—God's Plan for Exciting Sexual Intimacy in Marriage, by Sam Laing.
Faith and Finances, by Patrick Blair.
Friends & Lovers—Marriage as God Designed It, by Sam and Geri Laing.
Mighty Man of God—A Return to the Glory of Manhood, by Sam Laing.
Pure the Journey—A Radical Journey to a Pure Heart, by David and Robin Weidner.
Raising Awesome Kids—Being the Great Influence in Your Kids' Lives by Sam and Geri Laing.
~ ¹ᵃ⁻ciple-Centered Parenting, by Douglas and Vicki Jacoby.
ial 8 Principles of a Growing Christian Marriage, by Sam and Geri Laing.
tial 8 Principles of a Strong Family, by Sam and Geri Laing.
—A Call to Every Man Everywhere, by Sam Laing.

Books by Curt Simmons—Available at www.ipibooks.com

Books by Curt Simmons—Available at www.ipibooks.com

For additional books go to
www.ipibooks.com